Frederick County Maryland Land Records
1771-1773

Liber P Abstracts, 1772-1773

(with a few deeds from 1771 mixed in)

Libers S-T-U – more 1773 deeds

Brief Abstracts for Indexing

compiled by:

Patricia Abelard Andersen

Damascus, MD

GenLaw Resources
26810 Grace Court
Damascus, Maryland 20872

INTRODUCTION TO FREDERICK COUNTY LAND RECORD ABSTRACTS

This volume includes Liber P which continues a series of abstracts begun in 1995 with Liber B, the first volume of deeds recorded in Frederick County, and also includes Abstract Indexes for Libers S, T and U. There were no Libers Q or R in Frederick County Deeds. The dates covered in these three volumes overlap, so it seems appropriate to include them in one book. The type of indexing available in abstracts cannot be replaced with the indexes available, that were prepared by the Circuit Clerks to identify property owners, and to assist the clerks in land property records. Users of these volumes understand much more is involved. The courts indexes do not always identify estate sales, bills of sale, Negro sales or manumissions, or depositions and information within deeds, such as deed boundaries with neighbors, and other documents brought to the court to be recorded. Also, many researchers have difficulty reading the old hand written books, so this also provides a guide and finding aid for the beginning genealogist. The page numbers of the deeds in the original volume are given in the abstracts. Since deeds have been put online at the Maryland State Archives Web Site, the serious researcher is encouraged to obtain copies of deeds of interest.

Abstracts are best used as brief guides and indexes to original records, and at the same time, to find people mentioned in deeds who would otherwise be lost in the records. This series of abstracts focuses on the names of parties in the deeds; the name of witnesses, when recognized as the usual Justices of the Peace are frequently omitted in these abstracts, nor was the paid alienation fine (always collected) noted in all cases. In most cases the metes and bounds were not detailed, although a few of these abstracts do contain more information; in all cases where it is desired to draw the tract out, the researcher is encouraged to print out an original deed to use.

In addition to the county court land records, some deeds were recorded in the Provincial Court land office. If someone had business at the Provincial Court, e.g. recording the certificate or obtaining their patent or a warrant to survey or resurvey land, it may have been more convenient for them to record their deeds at the state level, instead of in the counties. They cover the colonial period and should always be checked when a transaction cannot be found recorded at the local level.

Any contract (indenture) may be recorded for real or personal property, or for services, if the contracting parties presented the indenture for recording. Most deeds were presented to the clerk for recording during Court Days, when the justices were in town. At this time all deeds were acknowledged before two justices of the peace, or other court officials, and in most instances these justices were also the witnesses. An annotated list of Justices of the Peace active during this period, follows. Bills of sale did not require witnesses to be justices, so they were more likely to be neighbors or family members. It appears that when deeds were made on other than court days, the parties went to the homes of the nearest Justices of the Peace, and in those instances you may find that the Justice enlisted other members of his family to serve as witnesses.

At the time of acknowledgment of the deed, the wife generally released her right to a 1/3 life interest in her husband's real property, referred to as her dower rights. Occasionally, she would come in later and record a separate release of dower. Widows, and mothers of sons inheriting property, also had dower rights to release. Deeds made and recorded during court days, were probably agreed to much earlier. These were more or less, universal "settlement" dates, convenient since most people came to court on court dates. Colonials were knowledgeable about the function of law, and the actions of the courts as they witnessed trials first hand. In colonial days, everyone who could, attended the live dramas offered by the quarterly sessions. Court days in Frederick County were the third Tuesdays of the months of March, June, August and November. The court would meet for several days, and could schedule meetings for several days as required. It is probable that the clerks or their assistants, then took the "recorded" deeds home with them to write up as time allowed. Witness the sign off of Liber U: by Geo M. Tyler, Apt. Clerk. After recording, the deeds could be picked up and the court record annotated as to who received the deed and what date, sometimes years later.

The signature may differ from the names as recorded in the deed. It was not uncommon for a name to be spelled in a different way three or more times within one document. In the abstracts, the name is spelled consistent with the clerk's spelling. If the family is known to the abstractor, the name may appear in the index only under the most common spelling. The index records only one entry per page, even when there may be several deeds for the party. The clerks were able to read and write a German Script, and when the original deeds' grantor, or witnesses signed the deed in German Script, the clerk copied the signature in German Script. He also apparently tried to copy marks as they appeared. However, all signatures in the deed book, were written in the handwriting of the clerk, therefore comparing these signatures from a deed book: one John Smith to another John Smith and saying the signatures were the same; does not imply that it was really the same John Smith or the same signatures on the original deed. Occupations will sometimes help distinguish a man. These are included in the abstracts and the more unusual occupations are indexed in this volume, except for the common "status indicators," of gentleman, planter, yeoman, and farmer. Also be aware that because of spelling inconsistencies, read the index to the volume carefully, looking for possible misreading and/or misspellings in the original, and variant spellings. Be especially vigilant for surnames beginning with "B" or "P". Abbreviations were frequently used in the Record Books. Some of them are also used in these abstracts. Names commonly abbreviated include: Abra'm (Abraham), Alex. (Alexander), Arch'd (Archibald), Benj. (Benjamin), Chas. (Charles), Dan'l (Daniel), Ign's (Ignatius), Jas (James), Jos. (Joseph), Jno. (John), Marg't (Margaret), Morda. (Mordecai), Nath'l (Nathaniel), Nin. (Ninian), Pris'a (Priscilla), Rich'd (Richard), Rob't (Robert), Sam'l (Samuel)., Thos. (Thomas), and Wm. (William).

List of Terms and Abbreviations Used in the Abstracts

AAC	Anne Arundel County
ack	Acknowledgment of the deed by the grantor.
afd/afs'd	aforesaid
AF	Alienation fine. A transfer fee.
BC	Baltimore County
Certificate of Survey:	After a warrant was obtained for land, a settler would contact a surveyor to have an official description of his real estate made. This was presented to the court to obtain a patent.
Commission:	A court order to individuals, as recorded in the deed books, these were generally to resurvey or remark to perpetuate the boundaries of a tract of

land where parties may have been in disagreement, or the original bounded trees fallen or in dispute.

Consideration
A required element of a contract, it is what the seller receives to induce him to make a bargain.

dower rights:
A wife or a widow's right to 1/3 of all her husband's real property. This right had to be released whenever he sold property. If not done at the time the deed was made, the widow could come back later and exercise a claim against the property, and sometimes later dower releases were recorded.

draught/draft:
One of the upper branches of a river or creek.

Fieri facias (Fi. Fa.)
Judicial writ directing sheriff to satisfy a judgment from debtors property.

FC
Frederick County

GS
German Script, in reference to a signature.

Hundred
as in Antietam Hundred, A unit for taxation purposes.

Indenture:
Any written contract. "Indentured servants" comes from this document.

lbs. tob.
Pounds of tobacco. (Legal money in Maryland)

M&B
Metes and bounds - description of real estate boundaries.

Manor of Monocacy
[or Calverton] - A unit of government similar to the Hundred, referred to in deeds, as to be held of the "Manor of Conecocheague" for example. It does not mean that the land was physically located within the manor survey. The land was in that taxing district for collection or quit rents.

patent
The original land grant from the Lord Proprietary, issued after a certificate of survey was made and returned.

PGC
Prince George's County

pistole
a gold coin used in various European countries.

rsy/rsy'd
resurvey/resurveyed

SMC
St. Mary's County

supersedeas
In some instances use is synonymous with a "stay of proceedings." Here it is most similar to a bond required of one who petitions to set aside a judgment or execution and from which the other party may be made whole if the action is unsuccessful.

JUSTICES OF THE FREDERICK COURT
& OTHER OFFICIALS ACTIVE IN THIS VOLUME (1773)

BAYNES, John. (1726-1790). He was a resident of Prince George's County.[1] Frequent witness to deeds for Georgetown lots.

BEALL, Samuel aka, Sam'l Beall Jr. (1713-1778). Resided on *Kelly's Purchase*, now Washington Co.. He served as justice from 1763-1775, the son of John Beall of Alexander and Verlinda Magruder Beall. Samuel Beall Jr. Married Eleanor Brooke and was the father of Brooke

---

[1] 1Henry C. Peden, Jr., *Revolutionary Patriots of Prince George's County, 1775-1783,* Westminster, Md., Family Line Publications, 1997, pg. 18.

Beall of Georgetown, and grandfather of Upton Beall, both clerks of the Montgomery County Court. He was younger than Samuel Beall, son of Ninian, grandson of Col. Ninian, who took the name Samuel Beall Sr. and married Jane Edmonston.[2] He was one of the "Twelve Immortal Justices of the Frederick County Court, who repudiated the Stamp Act - November 23, 1765" celebrated on a plaque in the Frederick County Courthouse.

BEALL, William Murdock (1742-1823), son of Nathaniel and Ann (Murdock) Beall. He resided in Frederick Town. From 1770 he served as Frederick County Clerk of Court receiving alienation fines on recording deeds. Justice in Frederick County, 1777 to at least 1794.[3]

BEATTY, Charles (1736-1804). He lived in Georgetown, Montgomery County and was the son of Thomas Beatty, and brother of Justice Thomas Beatty Jr. He was married twice, first to Mary Middagh and second to Verlinda Offutt. He served in the Lower House of the Legislature from Frederick County in 1771.[4] He was a land speculator who sold lots in Georgetown in partnership with George Frazer Hawkins.

BLAIR, Willliam (1730-1778). Served as justice from at least 1767; on Committee of Correspondence, and as an associator from Tom's Creek Hundred.[5] His will filed in Frederick County named a wife and several children.[6] He was one of the twelve justices of the Frederick County Court, who repudiated the Stamp Act - November 23, 1765.

BURGESS, Edward. (1733-1809) . He was born in Anne Arundel County, and married Mary Davis, daughter of Thomas Davis and Elizabeth Gaither. Around 1773, he moved into thelower district of Frederick County and became involved in politics. He was an Anti-Federalist. He was a Justice of Frederick County, and held the same position in Montgomery County, at its formation. He was elected a representative to the Lower House of the Maryland Assembly ten times from 1777 to 1799. In 1776, he became a Captain in the Flying Camp of Revolutionary War soldiers. He settled near Logtown on the left side of the road from Georgetown to Frederick, somewhere near today's Gaithersburg High School. *Belt's Desire.* He also owned other real property, some with improvements. Between 1779 and 1790 he purchased about 1200 acres of land, much of this land was attached and sold by court order between 1792 and 1798 for debts. Therefore Edward Burgess was a prime example of the type of person who could take up the Anti-Federalist cause. He had debts which the issuance of paper money might help to alleviate.[7]

---

[2] Edward C. Papenfuse, Alan F. Day, David W. Jordan and Gregory A. Stiverson, *A Biographical Dictionary of the Maryland Legislature, 1635-1789. 2 vols.* (Baltimore: Johns Hopkins University Press, 1797, 1985) pg. 124; Eleanor M.V. Cook, *The Brooke Beall Family and the John's Family,* mss. dated July 1986, copies at the Maryland State Archives and Montgomery County Historical Society; also, Nettie Leith Major, "Ninian Beall, 1625-1717" in *MGSB,* Summer 1979, vol. 20, #3, pg. 214-225.

[3] Papenfuse, et.al., op.cit., pg. 125-126.

[4] Ibid., pg. 126-127.

[5] Henry C. Peden, Jr., *Revolutionary Patriots of Frederick County, 1775-1783,* Westminster, Md., Family Line Publications, 1995, pg. 38.

[6] Abstracted in *Western Maryland Genealogy,* vol. 5:132.

[7] *Montgomery County Story,* Vol. 30, no. 2, pg. 273.

CAMPBELL, Aeneas (Aens, other abbreviations) (1730-1812). He was born in St. Mary's County, Maryland, moved to Leesburg area in Loudoun County in 1757, and then into Frederick County around 1765. He lived on tracts in Sugarland Hundred which became a part of Montgomery County in 1776.

CHAPLINE, Joseph (1746-1821), with brothers James and William, sons of Justice Joseph Chapline (1707-1769) are active in this volume, selling lots in Sharpsburg, and other real estate they inherited in the Antietam Valley.[8] He lived at *Mt. Pleasant* near Sharpsburg, and pursued a legal career in Frederick Town.

CRESAP, Michael (1742-1775) son of Justice Thomas Cresap (1703-1788), served as witness in this volume, he lived in Western Maryland, in part of county which became Washington County.[9]

CRESAP, Thomas, Justice from March Court 1748/9.[10] b. 1703 Skipton, Yorkshire, d. 1788. He acted as Maryland's agent to the Cherokee and Iroquois Indians, and settled out at Old Town on the Potomac River, now Allegany Co. He was a Justice of Prince George's County from 1739-1748, and served Frederick County as a Justice from 1748 through 1775, as well as in other capacities, including as deputy surveyor. [Papenfuse, p.244]

DEAKINS, William Jr. (1742-1798). Served as Justice of the Peace in Frederick, and then Montgomery Counties.

DUCKETT, Richard Jr (1732-before 1803) a resident and Justice of Prince George's County, married to Martha Waring.[11]

DULANEY, Benjamin. Clerk and Record Keeper of Frederick County, bonded 2 May 1773.

DULANEY, Daniel, Esq. Chief Justice, Frederick County Court. from March 1748/9 through 1751.[12] He died in 1753, and his sons Daniel Dulaney and Walter Dulaney, both of Anne Arundel County, are present in this volume, because of their extensive interests in Frederick Town lots and other Frederick County real estate.[13]

HAWKINS, George Fraser. (1741-1785). Son of John Hawkins (1713-1757). Resided in Prince George's County on Potomac River, opposite of Alexandria. Married to Susannah Trueman Somerville.[14] With Charles Beatty, developer of Georgetown lots.

---

[8] Papenfuse, op.cit., pg. 210-211.

[9] Henry C. Peden, *Revolutionary Patriots of Washington County, Maryland 1776-1783*, Westminster, Md., Family Line Publications, 1998, pg.83.

[10] Millard Millburn Rice, *This Was the Life: Excerpts from the Judgment Records of Frederick County, Maryland, 1748-1765*, Redwood City, CA: Monocacy Book Co., 1979, Appendix C, pg. 285.

[11] Peden, *Patriots of Prince Georges County*, pg. 94.

[12] Rice, op.cit.

[13] Papenfuse, et.al., op.cit., pgs. 284-289.

[14] Papenfuse, et.al., op.cit., pgs. 423-424.

HEPBURN, John. (d. 1775) Merchant of Upper Marlboro. A Proprietary Justice who often served as witness for residents selling property in Frederick County, in what is now the Montgomery County/Rock Creek and Silver Spring areas, where he owned parts of *Hermitage*, and over 2200 acres of *Hanover*.[15]

HEUGH, Andrew.(1727-1789) Served as a Justice from 1756[16] through at least 1775. Lived in Lower Potomac Hundred, Frederick County, which later became part of Montgomery County. Served in the Lower House of the Legislature, 1769-1770.[17]. Was one of the twelve justices who repudiated the Stamp Act, November 23, 1765.

JONES, Charles. (1712-1798). Served as a Justice from 1754.[18] He was one of the twelve justices of the Frederick County Court who repudiated the stamp act. He lived on *Clean Drinking Manor* on the west side of Rock Creek, just north of the present line with the District of Columbia. In 1777, he became the first judge of the Orphans Court of Montgomery County.[19]

JENIFER, Daniel of St. Thomas (1723-1790). Lived near Annapolis in Anne Arundel County, he was a Justice of the Provincial Court, 1766-1773 and appointed Rent Roll Keeper of the Western Shore in 1768. He also held other offices.[20]

LYNN, David (d. 1779) (first Grand Jury foreman 1748/9), served as Justice from 1754.[21] An immigrant from Dublin, Ireland, he was a Surveyor, and one of the Commissioners to lay out Georgetown in 1751, served as a Justice through 1775. David Lynn died before 16 December 1779, when Andrew Heugh and Roger Brooke prepared the inventory of his estate, filed 18 February 1780 in Montgomery County; David Lynn, was administrator, Sarah Lynn, Caty Lynn signed as next of kin.[22] He was also the father of John Lynn, who resided in Allegany (now Garrett County).[23] On 10 May 1790, his widow Elizabeth made her will, which was probated in Montgomery County 9 Sept. 1803.[24]

LOWNDES, Christopher (1713-1785). A well to do merchant who lived at *Bostwick* in Bladensburg, Prince George's County. He was married to Elizabeth Tasker and therefore, brother-in-law of Daniel Dulaney.[25]

---

[15] *Maryland Calendar of Wills, Vol. 16,* pg. 77-78.

[16] Rice, *op.cit.*

[17] Papenfuse, *op.cit.,* pg. 439.

[18] Rice, *op.cit.*

[19] Jones Family File, Montgomery County Historical Society Library, Rockville, Md.

[20] Papenfuse, *op.cit.,* 485-486.

[21] Rice, *op.cit.*

[22] Eleanor M. V. Cook, *Abstract of Estate Record Book Liber A, 1777-1780, Montgomery County, Maryland,* non-published manuscript, dated March 1993 at the library of the Montgomery County Historical Society, pg. 35.

[23] Papenfuse, *op.cit., pg 558.*

[24] Mary Gordon Malloy, Jane C. Sween, Janet D. Manuel, *Abstracts of Wills, Montgomery County, Maryland, 1776-1825,* Washington, D.C., Gray Printing Company, copyright by authors, 1977. Pg. 87.

[25] Peden, *Patriots of Prince Georges County*, pg. 194.

LUCKETT, William (1711-1783). He operated a ferry across the Potomac River to Virginia, which was later operated by his son-in-law, Thomas Noland. He was an Innholder in Frederick County by 1754 and served as a justice, intermittently from 1757 through 1775.[26]

PRATHER, Basil, witnessed several deeds with Thomas Prather below. Probably the one who received an equal share of the Thomas Prather estate.[27]

PRATHER, Thomas, (1704-1785) Justice from March Court 1748/9 through 1762. He was Sheriff in 1762, and served intermittently as Justice through 1775. He was a brother of John Smith Prather.[28] Jannet Prather was one of estate administrators in Washington County.[29] She also appeared as witness occasionally with him.

PRICE, Thomas (1732-1795). Served as a Justice of the Peace from 1758.[30] He was one of the twelve justices who repudiated the Stamp Act, November 23, 1765. He lived in Sugarland Hundred; his daughter Matilda Bowen Price, married Upton Beall 29 December 1796.

SCHLEY, Thomas (1712-1790). Emigrant from Germany, ca. 1743, paid quit rents to Daniel Dulaney on lots in Frederick Town from 1746, where he operated a tavern. In Germany he was the German Reformed School Master in Appenhofer for at least 10 years prior to emigrating.[31]

SHELBY, Evan. Served as a Justice of the Peace from 1763.[32] He lived near Hagerstown, but moved further west in 1772.

SMITH, Joseph. Served as Justice 1753 through 1759, and again 1763 on.[33] In 1775, he served on the Committee of Observation, until appointed Lt. Col. 36th Bn. Militia of Frederick County, and in 1778, became Col. Of Militia in Washington County.[34]

STEUART, Adam. Served as justice from at least 1772 in Frederick County, and later in Montgomery County. Often witnessing Georgetown transactions.

STULL, John. (1733-1791). Served as justice from at least 1772 in Frederick County. His home plantation, *Whiskey*, was located near Elizabethtown which, after division of county, became Hagerstown, the county seat for Washington County. His second wife was Mercy Williams, daughter of Joseph Williams, a tavern keeper. He was elected to the State Legistlature by 1775.[35]

---

[26] Papenfuse, *op.cit., pg. 553;* Harry Wright Newman, *The Lucketts of Port Tobacco.,* Washington, D.C., author, 1938.

[27] Peden, *Patriots of Washington County,* pg. 289, 290.

[28] Rice, op.cit.; Papenfuse, *op.cit.,* pg 659.

[29] Peden, *Patriots of Washington County,* pg 290.

[30] Rice, *op.cit.*

[31] Grace L. Tracey & John P. Dern, *Pioneers of Old Monocacy: The Early Settlement of Frederick County, Maryland, 1721-1743,* pgs. 150-151, 265-266.

[32] Rice, *op.cit.*

[33] Rice, *op.cit.*

[34] Peden, *Patriots of Frederick County,* pg. 341.

[35] Papenfuse, *op.cit.,* Vol. 2, pg 792.

WINCHESTER, William (1710-1790). Born in London, he emigrated to Annapolis in 1729 at age 19. Lived Pipe Creek Hundred. Acquired over 1000 acres of *White's Level,* and surveyed the town of Winchester in 1764, which today is Westminster, the Carroll County seat. Other names for the town included "New London Town," "Bedford," Grandadam Farm" and "Logsdon's Tavern Land."[36]

WOOD, Joseph. (d. 1772) Served as Justice from 1753.[37] Lived in Linganore Hundred from before 1748. Died testate in 1772 with issue. His wife Catherine Wood served as co-witness with him at times.[38]

WOOTTON, Thomas Sprigg (d. 1789). Son of Turner Wooton, by his last wife, Elizabeth Sprigg Wilson Wootton, the widow of Josiah Wilson, daughter of Col. Thomas Sprigg. Had legislative career in Lower House, 1769-1770. Served as a Justice of the Peace in Frederick County from 1768-1777, until county divided, then served in Legislature from Montgomery County.[39] He was married to Molly Offutt, who was murdered. No children. It was he who introduced the 31 August 1776 Resolution to create Montgomery County from lower Frederick County.[40]

[36] Nancy M. Warner, Ralph B. Levering and Margaret Taylor Woltz, *Carroll County Maryland: A History 1837-1976.* Caroll County Bicentennial Committee, 1976., g. 20, 34.

[37] Rice, *op.cit.*

[38] Peden, *Patriots of Frederick County,* pg. 402. Will abstracted in *Western Maryland Genealogy,* Vol. 6:30.

[39] Papenfuse, *op.cit.,* pg. 910.

[40] William N. Hurley, Jr., *Montgomery County Families, Volume II,* Bowie, Md.: Heritage Books, 2004, pg. 243. His source appears to be the Wootton family files, Montgomery County Historical Society, article by Emily Emerson Lantz, "Maryland Heraldry: Woottons of Prince Georges and Montgomery,*"* *Baltimore Sun*, 19 May 1907.

1-2. Martin Cassell recorded deed 19 April 1772, made 9 April, from Jacob Humbert for £700 sells two tracts, *Braden's Lott,* 100 acres, and one part of *Beatty's Venture,* 100 acres. Beginning on Wests Cabbin Branch, a draught of Israel's Creek. Signed before Jos Wood, Abraham Wood. Receipt. Elizabeth wife of Jacob Humbert released dower.

2-3. Henry Shover, blacksmith, recorded deed 19 April 1772, made 24 March from Fielder Gant of Frederick County, ironmaster. Sells part of *Fielderia Manor,* beginning at tract called *Baker's Ramble*, to 7 line of tract called *Chance.* Containing 200 acres. th Signed before Jos Wood, Thos Price.

4-5. Augustus Sharer, farmer, recorded deed 19 April 1772 from Jacob Richards of Taneytown, wheelwright, for £230 Pennsylvania currency, sells part of *Brother's Agreement.* Signed before Jos Wood, Conrad Boner. Catharine, wife of Jacob Richards released dower.

5-7. Elias Delasmith recorded deed 19 April 1772, made 24 March between Fielder Gantt for £18..14 sells part of *Fielderia Manor,* beginning at 15th line of tract *Children's Chance,* containing 100 acres. Signed before Jos Wood, Thos Price.

7-8. Edward Lamb recorded deed 19 April 1772, made 6 March from Charles Carroll, Esq., Senior of Anne Arundel County, sells tract in Frederick County called the *Resurvey on Locust March,* containing 230 acres. Whereas John Cove, John Reister and the said Edward Lamb, have purchased all the said tract of land. Signed before Dan'l of St. Thos Jennifer.

9-10. Henry Sailer recorded deed 19 April 1772 made 19 March 1772 from Samuel Tullebough, Dollerbaugh) for £150 Pennsylvania, *Resurvey on part of Chestnutt Hill,* to part of tract called *Tuskaroll Gap*, containing 100 acres more or less. Signed by mark before Jos Wood, Wm Luckett. Receipt. Acknowledgment. Catharine Tullebough released dower rights. [Script recording this deed is different than following script.]

10-11. Ignatius Perry recorded deed 13 May 1771. I Rachel Pottinger for the natural love and affection which I have for by beloved son, Ignatius Perry, and for 5 shillings, assign following parcels of land, called *Charles Purchase,* part of a tract called *Charles and William,* beginning at a large branch of Sligo, of Potomack River, purchased by my husband Charles Perry of Charles, William and John Beall containing 296 acres, 64 whereof begin at a tract which said husband Charles Perry purchased of Ninian Tannehill, beginning at a tract called *Fenwick.* Signed Rachel Pottinger, before Thos Sprigg, Richard Duckett Junr.

11-13. Isaac Johnson recorded lease 27 April 1772, made 15 April from Charles Carroll for rents and covenents herein, conveys part of tract *Aix la Chapelle,* metes and bounds given for 100 acres. To pay annual rents, first payment to be made in 1774, and he will build within 4 years one framed log tobacco house 32 ft by 20 ft. to be covered with lap shingles, and one framed dwelling house, not less than 20 ft. by 16 ft., covered with lap shingles, and also to plant 100 apple trees, and put in a good fence. Signed in the presence of Jona Slater, Charles Carroll Junr.

13-15. Thomas Johns and others (Thomas Richardson of Frederick County and Clement Biddle and John Biddle of Philadelphia, merchants) recorded deed 1 May 1772, made 24 April, from Benjamin Becraft Junior and Peter Becraft, for £118 sell tract called *Barsheba,* containing 5 ½ acres, and part of a tract called *Dan,* containing 16 acres on the west side of Rock Creek Branch, beginning at the beginning tree of a tact called *Joseph's Park,* on the east side of Rock Creek, to a parcel of land conveyed by Richard Beall to Peter Bartholomew, to a parcel belonging to John Ridgeway, to a parcel belonging to Edward Tucker purchased of Richard Beall, then to beginning laid out for 30 ¼ acres of land. Signed by Benjamin Becraft Junr. Peter Becraft, before Charles Jones, Andrew Heugh. On 24 April 1772 Richard Beall, son of Samuel having conveyed the within three parcels of land with the mill premises and appurtenances to the said Benjamin Becraft Junior and Peter Becraft, and Sarah the wife of Richard Beall, having never relinquished her right of dower to them, in the three parcels of land with the mill premises, she the said Sarah wife of Richard Beall, son of Samuel, acknowledged her dower rights. Mary wife of Peter Becraft also released her dower rights.

15-16. Daniel of Saint Thomas Jenifer, gentleman of the City of Annapolis, recorded deed 5 May 1772, made 23 Dec. 1771 from Samuel Hardisty of Frederick County, planter, for £50 part of tract of land called *Leaches Lot.* Signed before James Brooks, John Courts Jones. Receipt. Acknowledgment.

16. Henry Ash recorded mark 12 May 1771 of cattle, cut a piece off the right ear, left ear split, hogs with same mark. Signed Henry Ash, Mr. Sprigg please to record the above.

16-17. Mary Smith recorded deed 7 May 1772, made 22 April between Richard King Stevenson of Baltimore County, farmer, for £20 grants unto Mary Smith, her life time without any molestation and after her decease to her son Richard Smith, his heirs and assigns, 82 acres of land in Frederick County, but formerly called Baltimore County, part of a tract called *Good Will,* beginning on 15th line of the *Resurvey on Good Will*, it being the 1st line of Richard Stevenson Junior's land. Signed by mark, Richard King Stevenson before Abraham Wood. Jos Wood.

18. Joshua Richards recorded bill of sale 7 May 1772, from Stephen Richards Junr. of Frederick County for £70 sells one feather bed and furniture, one blue rug, one red ditto, 23 yards of woolen cloth, 33 pounds of flax and 8 pounds of woolen yarn; one woman's side saddle, one linen wheel, 12 pewter plates, 2 dishes one pewter basin, 2 iron pots, earthen plates, iron tools listed, other housewares enumerated, one gray horse, two cows described, also 17 acres of wheat now growing. Signed by mark Steven Richards before James Smith, Levi Carmack.

18-20. Charles Reynolds recorded deed 7 May 1772, made April 1772 between Joseph Smith, for £163 sells part of *Friendship Enlarged,* containing 103 acres. Signed before Andrew Heugh, David Lynn. Rachel, wife of Joseph released dower rights.

20-21. Alexander McLanagan recorded deed 7 May 1772 made 22 April between Isaac Baker for 43..12 sells part of *Resurvey on Pleasant Bottom,* Signed before Evan Shelby, Thomas Prather.

21-22. Christian Eversole recorded bill of sale 10 May 1772 from George Myres of Frederick County for £17 sells one dark brown gelding, provided nevertheless that if sum paid sale is void. Signed German script before Richard Davis

22-23. John Hunsacher recorded deed 18 May 1772 from David Stoner and Abraham Stoner both of Cumberland County, Pennsylvania. For £420 Pennsylvania sells tract, called *Resurvey on Content.* Signed before Thomas Prather, Thomas Brooke. Margaret and Mary the wives of said David and Abraham released dower rights.

23-24. Philemon Plummer recorded deed 9 May 1772, made 7 Nov 1771 between Samuel Mount for £30 land called *Pairpoints Range,* containing by estimation 63 acres. Signed by mark before William Hormus, Henry Barkshire.

24-25. Henry Leatherman recorded deed 7 May 1772, made 27 April between Daniel Dulaney of the City of Annapolis, and Walter Dulaney of the same place, executors of Daniel Dulaney Esq. for £85. Tract called *Maple Bottom.*

25-27. Conrad Hockersmith recorded deed 14 May 1772, made 14 November 1771, from Benjamin Biggs for £30 tract called *Resurvey on Benjamin's Luck,* containing 50 acres. Signed before William Blair, Jos. Wood. Margarita Prudence Deborah Margarita wife of Benjamin Biggs released dower rights.

27-28. Daniel Arnold recorded deed 7 May 1772, made 20 Nov. 1772 from Samuel Crable (Grable) for £136 sells tract called *Resurvey on Piney Grove,* containing 106 acres. Hannah Grable examined out of hearing of her husband released dower.

28-30. William Arnold and John Robinson Recorded lease 11 May 1772 from Charles Carroll Jr. For rents and covenents, two parts of tract of land called *Aix la Chapelle,* containing 75 acres, and the second part containing 75 acres. They agree to build a framed or log tobacco house, 32 ft by 20 ft. and also two framed dwelling houses, not less than 20 ft. by 16 ft. covered with lap shingles; also to plant on the premises 75 apple trees on each lot,

30-31. Philip Moody recorded mortgage 11 May 1772 from Philip Angleberger [Philip Hungleberry son of Philip] for £50 tract *Whimpenny Fell*[41] on north side of a branch that leads into Tuscarora Creek. Signed in German Script before Thomas Price, Michael Tabler. Receipt. Acknowledgment.

32-34. George Devilbiss recorded deed 17 May 1772 from Gabriel McKenzie for £310. For first, part of *Gabriel's Choice,* and part of the *Resurvey on Gabriel's Choice.* Containing 78 acres and the second part, originally granted Captain John White, and by him conveyed unto Gabriel McKenzie, beginning near the head of Little Pipe Creek, containing 50 acres. The third being a tract called *Addition to Gabriel's Choice,* granted Gabriel McKenzie, containing 19 acres. Signed by mark before Thomas Price, Rebecca Price. Sarah, wife of Gabriel McKenzie released dower rights.

34-36. Conrad Crush (Grosh) recorded deed 17 May 1772, made 24 March, from Fielder Gantt for £9..4 sells part of *Fielderia Manor,* containing 150 acres. Signed before Jos Wood, Thomas Price.

36-40. Enoch Davis, miller, recorded deed 17 May 1772, made 12 April from Martin Cassell, of Frederick County, millwright, Whereas Joshua Owings of Baltimore County by his deed 14 Dec. 1762 for consideration therein granted unto the aforesaid Martain Cassell, all that tract of land called *Johannes Lott,* in Frederick County, and whereas John Phillips late of Frederick County, did by his

---

[41] Whimpenny, Wimpenny is a common English surname in Yorkshire, derives from a medieval nickname for a person who was eager to acquire material possessions. Peter Wilson Coldham in his series, *Settlers of Maryland, 1751-1765,* shows that Philip Angleberry patented "Winfinimtall" 29 Nov 1755, in Frederick County.

deed 28 June 1769, for consideration there in did grant unto Martin Cassell that tract being part of land called the *Resurvey on Laugh and be Fat,* metes and bounds given containing 2 ½ acres of land; now this indenture witnesseth that in consideration of the sum of £859..2 he grants the said tracts, Also with the tract of land containing 2 ½ acres with all messuages, tenements, improvements, water courses and privileges. Signed German script before George Murdock, Thos Price.

40-42. Joseph Wright and Allen Farquhar recorded deed 7 May 1772, made 6 Nov. 1771 from William Farquhar, farmer of Pipe Creek. Whereas Frederick, Lord Proprietor did grant 21 April 1756 unto William Farquhar the elder father of the aforesaid William Farquhar Junr. A certain tract of land called *Resurvey on Forest,* containing 757 acres of land, recorded in Liber BC&GS No. 6, folio 283; and the said William Farquhar, the elder by his deed conveyed to his son the aforesaid William Farquhar Junr. a certain piece of said land, now this indenture, in consideration of the sum of 5 shillings grants for the use and benefit of the people called Quakers to erect a meeting house, to worship, and for a burying ground, all the following described tract or parcel of land, part conveyed to him by his father William Farquahar, beginning at a marked black oak standing in the 3rd line of the land conveyed to him on the east side of the hill near to the great road, running thence, metes and bounds given for 2 acres of land. Signed in the presence of William Blair, William Farquhar.

42-44 Daniel Stevenson recorded deed 7 May 1771, from Richard King Stevenson of Baltimore County, farmer, for £100 sells 150 acres of land in Frederick County, but formerly called Baltimore County, called *Goodwill.* Signed by mark befoer Jos Wood, Abraham Wood.

44-46. Nicodemas Bond recorded deed 17 May 1772 from Richard King Stevenson for £25 grants part of tract called *Resurvey on Goodwill,* to the given line of Edward Stevenson's part of said land. Signed by mark before Jos Wood, Abraham Wood.

46-48. George Clingan of Donegal Township, Lancster County, recorded deed 22 May 1772, made 21 May 1772 between John Hall of Frederick County for £1650 Pennsylvania, sells part of tract called *Carroll's Delight,* being in Fredeick County, at a corner of John Withrow's plantation, next to the mountain, containing 375 acres more or less. John Hall signed before Jos Wood, Abrahm Taylor. Elizabeth, wife of John Hall released dower before Jos Wood, Thos Price.

48-50. Flayle Payne recorded deed 17 May 1772, maded 27 April between Peter Payne of Frederick County, for £100 sells part of tract of land called *Pain's Delight,* being part of a tract of land bequqthed to him the said Peter Payne by his father Flayll Payne, as by the last will and testament among the records of the Prerogative Office in Frederick County. Signed by mark, before William Luckett, William Fennimore. Elizabeth Payne, wife of Peter Payne released dower.

50-53. William Farquhar recorded deed 7 May 1772, made 6 Nov. 1771 from William Farquhar the elder, to his son. *Resurvey on Forrest in Need,* 757 acres recorded in patents, for the natural love and affection and for the sum of 5 shillings, he sells to him two several tracts of land. The other called *The Resurvey on Mount Pleasant,* containing 70 ½ acres. Signed before Wm Blair, Allen Farquhar.

"FOR WANT OF ROOM in the proceeding record, the few remaining deeds in 1771 are recorded to Folio 78 - when deeds for 1772 Proceeds in course."

53-55. Thos Johnson recorded deed 23 Dec. 1771, made 20 Dec. 1771 between Tobias Horyne, for £81 parcel called *Sehen Taler Gutt,* beginning at a draught of mill creek, near tract of land called

Johnsons Lane, between elder surveys. Signed in German script before Saml Beall Junr. Thos Price. Receipt.

55-56. Charles Jones recorded deed 23 Dec. 1771 from Henry Wilson for £5 sterling, sells tract, part of *Grubby Thickett*, beginning at a white oak, at the start of a tract called *White Oak Valley*, containing 46 ½ acres. Signed before David Lynn, Andrew Heugh. Philander, wife of Henry Wilson released dower rights.

56-58. Martin Keplinger recorded deed 23 Dec. 1771, made 16 Dec. Between Henry Hunter of Frederick Co., for £200 sells tract called *Leeds*, within 1/4 mile of the foot of Kittoctin Mountain containing 50 acres, and part of the *Resurvey on Johnson's Levell*, adjacent to *Leeds*, containing 150 acres. Deed acknowledged by Henry Hunter. Before Sam Town Rigby and Charles Beatty. At the same time, Mary Ann Helms, wife of John Helms, who having a right of dower in the within mentioned land, examined apart and released dower.

58-59. Christian Stouder recorded deed 23 Dec. 1771, made 20 Nov. Between Benjamin Ridge of Frederick County, for £15 sells tract called *Benjamin's Choice*, on north side of Monocacy near a tract called *Pawpaw Bottom*, Signed before Jos. Wood, Thos Price. Catharine Ridge, wife of Benjamin released dower rights.

59-60 Peter Englar recorded deed 23 Dec. 1771, made 10 Dec. Between John Weaver for £150 sells lot in Frederick Town #50. Signed German script before Jos Wood, Thos Price. Elizabeth Weaver released dower rights.

61-62. Valentine Myers recorded deed 23 Dec. 1771, made 9 Dec. Between Alexander Esteb, for £110 sells part of a tract called *Beall's Manor*, beginning at end of Gerard Davis's first line, containing 100 acres. Signed before David Lynn, Andrew Heugh.

62-63. Valentine Eiler recorded deed 23 Dec. 1771, made 17 Dec. Between Wm Goodman of Frederick County, carpenter, for £12 part of tract of land called *Resurvey on Cooper's Alley*, containing 25 acres. Signed German script before Saml Beall Jr., Wm Blair. Penelope Goodman released dower rights.

63-65. Michael Arthur (Erter) recorded deed 23 Dec 1771, made 23 Nov. from Martin Winters, for £5 sterling, sells part of tract by name of *Addition to Resurvey to Stockstills Hills*, beginning at a tract called *Talkers Care*, Signed German Script before Thos Price, Jno Kuhn. Receipt. Mary the wife of Martin Winter released dower rights.

65-66. Henry Albright recorded deed 23 Dec. 1771, made 19 Dec. 1771 from Thomas Gilbert for £12 sells parcel called the *Pelican*, containing 11 ½ acres. Signed before Wm Blair, Charles Jones. Elizabeth Gilbert released dower rights.

66-67. Thomas Newswanker recorded deed 23 Dec. 1771, made 18 Nov. Between Danl Dulaney and Walter Dulaney of the City of Annapolis, executors of Daniel Dulaney deceased for £115 sells tract called *Watson's Folly*, a mile from the mountains in the head of the Cat Tail Meadows a draught of Antietam, Signed before Danl of St. Thos Jennifer.

67-68. Zachariah White recorded deed 23 Dec. 1771 from Joseph Stallings Jr., made 114 March 1771 for 5 shillings sterling, assigns parcel called *Grove's Hunting Out Lot*, metes and bounds given, containing 36 acres of land. Signed before Andrew Heugh, Charles Jones.

68-70. James Norwood of Anne Arundel County, recorded deed 23 Dec. 1771, made 17 Dec. 1771 between Green Spurrier of Frederick County, for £300 sells his right to tract called *Friendship,* beginning 51 perches in the last line of the said land, metes and bounds given for 300 acres more or less. Signed by Green Spurrier before Jno Wood, Andrew Heugh. Abuss hers[42] wife of Green Spurrier released dower rights. Signed and acknowledged before above.

70. Richard Holland recorded deed 23 Dec. 1771 from Ephraim Howard made 14 Dec. 1771 for £3..10 sells parcel called *Lap Land,* containing 12 ½ acres, beginning at a tract called *Rich Hills,* Signed before Thos Price, Eneas Campbell. Acknowledgment. Receipt.

70-72. Joseph Wilson recorded deed 23 Dec. 1771, made 26 Oct. 1771, from John Lamar of the Colony of Georgia, and Robt Lamar of the Province of South Carolina, for 5 shillings assigns part of tract called *Conclusion,* and part of another tract called the *Joseph & James,* containing 19 acres; and part of a tract called *Two Brothers,* containing 37 acres, all within the metes and bounds of the original lines of the tract aforesaid, in the whole 76 ½ acres. Signed in the presence of Jno Suter, Thos Richardson, Thos Lamar. Leonard Davis of Frederick County was appointed lawful attorney for Jno LaMar and Robt LaMar.

72-73. Daniel and Samuel Hughes recorded deed 23 Dec. 1771, made 14 Dec. 1771, from William Paca of the City of Annapolis, attorney of the one part, for £400 sells tract called *Resurvey on the Three Springs,* containing 1660 acres, all part of *Resurvey on Waggoner's Fancy,* containing 397 acres. Signed by William Paca, Mary Paca released dower. Wm Stewart, Charles Wallace, Rob Cowan, Wm M. Beall witnesses.

73-75. Joseph Peak, minister of the Gospel, recorded deed 23 Dec. 1771, made 7 Oct. 1771, from Andrew Park and Abraham Hayter, both of Frederick County, for £280 sells tract a part of *Addition to Brooke Discovery on the Rich Lands,* beginning at the end of 266 perches in the first course, made over by James Brooke to Abraham Hayter, Signed before Wm Blair, Alexr Shannon. Susanna Hayter wife of Abraham released right of dower.

75. Doctor Philip Thomas recorded lease 24 Dec. 1771, made 26 March 1771 between Michael Ramer, Jno Shelman, Christopher Edelin and Casper Shaaff all of Frederick Town, for 7 shillings sterling, lets all that stone messuage or tenement and lot of land, known by number 30 in the plat of Frederick Town, being only part of the said lot number, paying the rent of one pepper corn if the same be lawfully demanded, the intent of these presents, of use into possession of the said Philip Thomas. Signed before Evan Shelby, Eneas Campbell.

76-77. Doctor Philip Thomas recorded release 24 Dec. 1771 from Michael Ramer, Jno Shelman, Christopher Edelin and Casper Shaaf, whereas by indenture dated 14 March 1759, recorded in Frederick County a certain Valentine Shroiner and Michael Ramer and Jno Shelman of the same place for £400 release is signed. Acknowledgment. Charlotte Ramer, Marg Shelman, Rebecca Edelin and Alice Shaaf relinquished any rights.

78. Christopher Edelen recorded deed 22 Dec. 1771, made 22 March 1771, from Doctor Philip Thomas for £542 sell and confirms parcel in Frederick town, lot #30, with the stone messuages or

---

[42] According to Peden's *Patriots of Anne Arundel County,* Green Spurrier was married to Avis Leaks. The name above does not appear legible, but could be some form of Avis.

tenement, together with improvements, Signed by Philip Thomas, Christopher Edelin before Evan Shelby, Ens Campbell. Receipt. Acknowledgment.

78-81. Joseph and Mary Wright his wife, recorded deed 7 May 1772, made 4 Nov. 1771 from William Farquhar, to Mary Wright his daughter and Joseph Wright. Whereas Charles, the Lord Proprietor, by his patent on 14 March 1731 granted a certain Jno Traddone, a tract on Little Pipe Creek, called *Kilfadda,* containing 200 acres, conveyed to the aforesaid Wm Farquhar. Also a parent 24 April 1754 granted Wm Farquhar a tract called *The Fancy,* containing 195 acres to him; in consideration of the natural love and affection he has for Joseph Wright and Mary his wife, and for 5 shillings, he assigns tracts. Metes and bounds given excepting only a burial place.

81-82. George Noble recorded deed 29 May 1772 from Zachariah Wade of Prince George's County, and Ann his wife, the daughter of George Noble of said County, deceased. Whereas Ann, by virtue of the last will and testament of the above George Noble her father, became seized in fee of a moiety or half part of a tract now lying in Frederick County, containing 85 acres more or less, assign to George Noble. Signed before Jno Baynes, Geo Hardy Junr.

82-83. Philip Coon recorded deed 27 May 1772, made 13 May, from Felix Morgan of Frederick County, for £25 sells part of parcel called *Pleasant Valley,* lying on the east side of the road from Frederick Town to Rhodrocks, containing 50 acres. Signed by mark before Thos Price, Conrad Hergerder (in German Script). Receipt. Acknowledgment.

84-85. Stephen Brunner, tanner, recorded deed 27 May 1772 from John Shriver for £100 sells part of a tract called *Second Resurvey on William's Pleasure,* metes and bounds given, for 100 acres. Signed by mark before Jos Wood, Thomas Price. Margaret, wife of John Shroyer released dower rights.

85-87. James Caldwell of York County, Pennsylvania, recorded deed 27 May 1772, made 12 May 1772, from Matthew Elder of Frederick County, for £600 sells tract called *Damhead,* formerly trasnferred from Michael Legat to James Jack, and from James Jack to the said Mathew Elder, metes and bounds given for 214 acres. Signed before Wm Blair, Elizabeth Blair. Mary, wife of Mathew Elder released dower rights before Wm Blair, Jos Wood.

87-88. Hance Vandal Hoover, blacksmith, recorded deed 27 May 1772 from John Shroyer sells part of tract, *Second Resurvey on William's Pleasure,* containing 69 ½ acres more or less. Margaret Shroyer released dower rights.

88-90. Stephen Brunner recorded deed 27 May 1772, made 12 May, from Conrad Hockersmith for £100 sells parcel by the name of *Samuel's Grievances,* laid out for 25 acres. Signed by mark before Jos Wood, Thos Price. Receipt. Acknowledgment. Maria Christiana Hockersmith, wife of Contrad released dower rights.

90-92. Michael Hockersmith recorded deed 27 May 1772 from John Shroyer for £20 sells and assigns part of *Second Resurvey on William's Pleasure,* metes and bounds given for 200 acres. Signed by mark before Jos Wood, Thos Price. Receipt. Acknowledgment. Margaret Shroyer released dower rights.

92-94. Jno Tracksal recorded deed 27 May 1772, from Jno Shroyer of Frederick County, for £265 sells part of *Second Resurvey on William's Pleasure,* metes and bounds given containing 131 acres, with improvements, signed by mark. Receipt, acknowledgment. Margaret Shroyer released dower rights.

94-95. Balser Moody recorded deed 27 May 1772, made 22 April 1772, from George Gillespy for £100 sells tract called *Neglect,* granted a certain Henry Benime, 5 Oct 1761, beginning on the east side of a draught that leads to the Potomac River, about ½ mile above *Jackson's Bottom,* and about 1/4 mile from the River, containing 75 acres. Signed before Evan Shelby, Thos Prather. Martha Gillespy released dower rights.

95-96. Rudolph Ply recorded deed 27 May 1772 from Paul Chrisman lot in Elizabeth Town, 82 ft. by 240 ft. paying yearly rents to Jonathan Hager. The wife of Paul Christ, named Madelina released dower rights.

96-97. Michael Dutterer Jr. Recored deed 27 May 1772 from Melchor Heffner for £260 sells tract called *Peace,* being a resurvey on a tract called *Stony Hills,* and part of a tract called *New Germany,* at the third line of *Resurvey on Stony Hills and Shoemaker's Choice,* containing 125 acres. Signed by mark before Jos Wood, Jno Wood. Receipt. Catharine, wife of Melchor Heffner released dower rights.

97-99. Casper Hoffman recorded deed 27 May 1772 from George Gillespy, made 22 April for £22 sells and grants land called *Huffman's part of Gillespy's Bargain,* metes and bounds given for 37 ½ acres. Signed before Evan Shelby, Thos Prather. Receipt. Acknowledgment. Martha Gillespie released doer rights.

99-100. John Fletchall recorded deed 27 May 1772 from William Rider, made 20 April, for £16 sells tract called *Trinity,* beginning at bounded red oak near head of a small Branch on the west fork of the Horse Pen Branch, which leads into the Sugar Lands, containing 9 acres more or less. Signed Wm Ryder before Andrew Huges, Eneas Campbell. Receipt. Acknowledgment. Sarah Ryder released dower rights.

100-101. Phillip Rimels recorded deed 27 May 1772, made 8 May between Frederick Nichodemus of Frederick County, for £26 sells 13 acres, part of land called *Coaliers Amendment*, metes and bounds given. Signed in German Script before Thomas Prather, Evan Shelby. Catharine, wife of Frederick Nichodemus released dower rights.

101-102. Jacob Crumbacher recorded deed 27 May 1772, made 19 May from Robert Burchfield, weaver. For £500 assigns three following parcels. *Roberts Purchase,* the *Crooked Piece,* and *the Resurvey on the Crooked Piece,* now called *Robert's Care All,* on the draughts of Sams Creek. Metes and bounds for 240 acres. Signed by mark before Jos Wood, Catharine Wood. Elizabeth wife of Robert Burchfield released dower rights.

103-104. Henry Carlow recorded deed 27 May 1772 from George Gillaspy made 24 April for £330 sells parcel, part of *Gillespies Bargain,* granted to said George Gillespy Senr. By patent . Metes and bounds for 223 acres. Signed before Evan Shelby, Thomas Prather. Martha Gillespy released dower rights

104-106. George Gaul recorded deed 27 May 1772 from George Gillespy for £215..16 sells two tracts, bginning to include the first tract or parcel, part of the *Resurvey on Ill Will,* granted to said George Gillespie Senr., 20 Dec. 1769 containing 111 acres; also all that other tract part of *Gillispies*

Bargain, containing 40 acres more or less. Signed before Evan Shelby, Thomas Prather. Martha Gillespy released dower rights

106-107. Casper Myer recorded deed 27 May 1772, made 12 May between Jacob Spagt, son and heir at law of Jacob Spagt of Frederick County, deceased. For £149 sells lot in Frederick Town, number 114, 80 ft. by 393 ft., with buildings, and advantages, the said lot, to pay 4 shillings yearly ground rent. Signed before Jos Wood, Thos Price. Receipt.

107-108. Samuel Magruder recorded deed 27 May 1772 from Nicholas Finck, taylor, for £132 sells parcel called *Goose Capp,* beginning at a tract called *The Forrest,* containing 62 1/4 acres. Signed in German Script before C. Beatty, Geo Walker. Receipt. Acknowledgment.

109-110. Jno Schades recorded deed 27 May 1772, made 12 May between Jno Reimberger, for £70 sells tract called *The Good Wife,* beginning at a bound hickory on the west side of a branch that falls into Tuscororah, which falls into Monocacy, about 16 perches and about 3/4 of a mile from Jacob Boks plantation, containing 87 acres. Signed in German Script before Jos Wood, Thos Price. Appolonia, acknowledged and relinquished her right of dower.

110-111. Samuel Carver recorded deed 13 June 1772, made 9 June from Leonard Kitzmiller for £370 sells tract called *Ivy Church,* beginning in the Beaver Dam Branch, a draught of Little Pipe Creek, to the end of the first part of Abraham Peaples part of said land, containing 102 ½ acres. Signed German Script, before Jos Wood, Jno Wood. Receipt. Acknowledgment. Hannah, wife of Leonard Kitzmiller, released dower rights.

111-112. Henry Snider recorded deed 13 June 1772, made 8 May between Frederick Nichodemas, farmer, for £40 sells 125 acres, part of a tract called *Collier's Amendment,* containing 120 acres more or less. Signed in German Script, in the presence of Thos Prather, Evan Shelby. Catharine, wife of Frederick Nichodemas released dower rights.

112-114. Leonard Miller recorded deed 13 June 1772, made 22 May between Jno Schoolfield of Baltimore County, for £100 Pennsylvania, sells a part of *Brooke's Discovery on the Rich Lands,* containing 100 acres, on the 9 line of tract of land James Brooke sold th to Jonah Dyer, which said Dyer sold to Jno Schoolfield. Signed before Jno Stewart (by mark) and Jonathan Doyle. Receipt. Rachel wife of Jno Schoolfield released dower rights.

114-115. Frederick Nichodemus recorded deed 13 June 1772, made 8 Mary between Jno McClellan of Cumberland County, Pennsylvania, farmer, for £50 Pennsylvania, sells parcel called *Brown's Grief,* standing on a great marsh known by the name of the Black Meadow, containing 30 acres according to the Certificate of Survey returned into the land office bearing date 28 August 1753. Signed before Thos Prather, Evan Shelby. Receipt. Martha McClellan released dower rights.

115-117. Thomas Wells of Baltimore County, recorded deed 13 June 1772 from James Wells, made 1 June for £5 sterling, sells parcel called the *Hollow Rock,* beginning on the south east side of Little Pipe Creek, containing 100 acres. Signed before Saml Owings, Deborah Owings.

117-118. Michael Snoufer recorded deed 13 June 1772 from Thomas Estep Junr. For £91 Pennsylvania, sells land called *Valleys & Hills, Tom's & Wills,* containing 45 acres. Signed by mark. Witness Jos Wood, Sam Wilson. Susanna wife of Thomas Estep released dower rights.

118-119. Peter Youdy recorded deed 13 June 1772 from Jacob Doll for £45 sells part of tract, *Park's Hall,* Signed before Saml Beall Junr., Thos Prather. Margaret Doll released dower rights.

119-121. Abraham Peaples recorded deed 13 June 1772, made 9 June from Leonard Kitzmiller, for £55 sells part of *Ivey Church,* containing 30 acres. Signed before Joseph Wood, Jno. Wood. Hannah wife of Leonard Kitzmiller released dower rights.

121-123. David Miller recorded deed 13 June 1772 from George Gillespy. Whereas David Gillespy, late of Frederick County deceased, being possessed in fee of a tract called *Gillespy's Purchase,* containing 100 acres, part of a tract called the *Three Friends,* being on the waters of Conococheague, that Geo Gillespy, abovementioned, being the eldest son and heir at law of the said David Gillespy, doth for the sum of £200 assigns tract metes and bounds given for 100 acres. Signed before Thos Prather, Evan Shelby. 7 May 1772, acknowledgment, and at the same time, came Jane Edmonston, who was left the widow of the within named David Gillespie deceased, being the mother of the aforesaid George Gillespy, and freely relinquished her right of dower.

123-124. Dan'l Sailer Junr. Recorded deed 13 June 1772, made 9 June between Leonard Kitzmiller, for £222 sells part of a tract called *Ivey Church,* containing 100 acres. Signed before Joseph Wood, Jno. Wood. Hannah wife of Leonard Kitzmiller released dower rights.

124-126. Wm Renner recorded deed 13 June 1772, from Balser Ream, for £210 sells part of *William's Gift,* containing 70 acres. Signed by mark before Jos Wood, Catherine Wood by mark. Catharine Reams wife of Balser Reams released dower rights.

126-128. David Miller recorded deed 13 June 1772 from Thomas Edmonsdon & Jean his wife for £100 sells parcel a part of *The Three Friends,* to a tract of land granted David Gelaspey, containing 12 acres of land. Signed Thomas Edmonston by his mark, Jane Edmonston by her mark. Before Thomas Prather, Evan Shelby. Deed acknowledged and dower rights released.

128-129. Henry Eller recorded deed 18 June 1772, made 9 June, from Leonard Kitzmiller for £167 part of *Ivey Church,* on Beaver Dam Branch of Little Pipe Creek, containing 110 acres. Signed in German script before Jos Wood, Jno Wood. Hannah Kitzmiller released dower.

130. Van Swearingen of Berly (Berkeley ?) County, Virginia, recorded on 7 June 1772, made same day deed from Joseph Chapline of Frederick County, lot #34 in Sharpsburg.

130-132. James Wells recorded deed 10 June 1772, made 1 June from Thomas Wells of Baltimore County for £6, part of tract called *Resurvey on Jacob's Wells,* signed before Saml Owings Jr., Deborah Owings. Elizabeth wife of Thomas Wells released dower rights.

132-134. Boston Knouff recorded deed 13 June 1772, made 9 June, from Leonard Kitzmiller for £182 sell part of *Ivey Church.* Signed in German script before Jos Wood, Jno Wood. Hannah Kitzmiller released dower.

134-135. Christian Eversole recorded deed 13 June 1772, made 28 Dec. 1771, from Jacob Eversole for tract called *Hellman's Look out,* containing 20 acres. Signed before Thos Prather, Saml Beall Junr. Mary, wife of Jacob Eversole released dower.

135-137. Leonard Kitzmiller recorded deed 13 June 1772, from Alexander Thomas, carpenter for £27 part of *Hammond's Strife,* 20 acres. Signature in German script, did not appear to be that of grantor. Catharine wife of Alexander Thomas released dower.

137-138. Michael Jumper recorded deed 13 June 1772, made 9 June, from Thomas Estep for £112..10 for tract *Kemp's Friend,* on line of *Valleys & Hills, Toms & Wills,* containing 49 ½ acres. Signed my mark. Susanna Estep released dower rights.

138-139. Ulrich Bruner recorded deed 13 June 1772, made 20 May 1772 from Daniel Robbins, for £60 sells parcel *Badham's Refuse,* near run on Israel's Cabbin Branch that falls into Potomac. Signed before Thomas Prather, Basil Prather.

140-141. Isaac Stallings recorded lease 16 June 1772 from Charles Carroll Jr., Esq. of Prince George's County, part of *Girl's Portion,* at first line of *Cloun Course*, containing 118 acres. Rent to be paid in tobacco at the Bladensburg Warehouse. To build within four years one good barn, and one framed dwelling house.

141-143. Isaac Stallings recorded lease 16 June 1772 from Charles Carroll Jr., Esq. of Prince George's County, part of *Girl's Portion,* to road that leads by Rob't Beall's plantation, containing 110 acres. Rent to be paid in tobacco at the Bladensburg Warehouse.

143-144. Thomas Trundell recorded lease 16 June 1772 from Charles Carroll Jr., Esq. of Prince George's County, part of *Girl's Portion,* during 21 years. Rent to be 1000 # tobacco in casque to be paid at the Bladensburg Warehouse. He is to keep the house now on premises in good repair, and to keep orchard now on premises in good order.

144-146. Thomas Trundell recorded lease 16 June 1772 from Charles Carroll Jr., Esq. of Prince George's County, part of *Girl's Portion,* during 21 years. Rent to be 1000 # tobacco in casque to be paid at the Bladensburg Warehouse. He is to build a framed tobacco house within 5 years.

146-147. Col. Greenbury Griffith recorded deed 16 June 1772 from Lodowick Davis for £284 sells *Resurvey on Benjamin's Square,* for 89 ½ acres. Signed before Charles Jones, David Lynn. Eleanor Davis released dower rights.

147-148. Balser Ream, tanner, and William Renner, recorded agreement 16 June 1772, made 5 June, on part of *Dutrow's lot*, on part of *Spring Plains*, regarding use of water 2 days after any four.

148-150. Agreement recorded June 1772, by Jno Tanner, son of Michael Tanner, with Michael Tanner and Eve his wife, in consideration of obligations and covenants, grants tract called *Miller's Chance,* and 50 acres of *Owing's Chance,* with improvement. John Tanner to provide yearly during their natural lives at their dwelling house in Taneytown, and should he outlive his parents, at their decease, John Tanner is to pay Andrew Tanner £20; and one year later he is to pay Michael Tanner, son of the above Michael Tanner £20 and one year following he is to pay Elizabeth Stomaker's heirs £20. Signed by the three parties.

150-158. William Hedges and Joseph Hedges recorded deed of partition 17 June 1772, made 14 June. By indenture made 15 March 1753, between Jacob Kneff of frederick County, heir at law of Jacob Kneff of Prince George's County, deceased, and the said Joseph and William Hedges, for considerations therein mentioned, tract called *Hedge Hog,* metes and bounds given for two parts containing 129 acres. Signed Jos Hedges, Wm Hedges before Thos Price, Chris Edelin. Mary wife of Joseph Hedges and Elizabeth wife of Wm Hedges released dower rights.

158-159. Robert Gassaway of Anne Arundel County, recorded deed 17 June 1772, made 14 June 1772, from Henry Griffith for £205..10 sells tract called *Nothing Ventured Nothing Got,* lying on east side of Monocacy near a tract called *Resurvey on Joseph's Friendship,* containing 100 acres more or less. Signed before Jos Wood, Chs Jones. Ruth Griffith released dower rights.

159-161. Peter and Benjamin Becraft recorded bargain of sale 17 June 1772, made 10 June 1772, from George Becraft for £700 Maryland, all that land whereon the said George Becraft lately inhabited, called *Sober Friendship,* 458 acres more or less, also all his real and personal estate of whatsoever nature, being all houses, out houses, edifices, buildings, gardens, orchards, subject nevertheless to one indenture of mortgage made of the said tract of land called *Sober Friendship* to Nicholas McCubbin of the City of Annapolis, for the payment of £200 and interest yielding and paying unto the right Honorable the Lord Proprietor. Signed by mark, Geo Becraft before Jos Wood, Thos Price. Elizabeth, wife of George Becraft released dower right.

161-163. Stephen West of Prince George's County, and Rachell Hall of Elk Ridge recorded deed 12 June 1772, made from John Dorsey of John of Frederick County. Whereas Jno Dorsey did heretofore mortgage unto a certain Harry Dorsey Gough the following tracts in Frederick County, *Resurvey on Mount Pleasant,* containing 1200 acres more or less, *Resurvey on Moab,* containing 455 acres and *Johns Good luck,* containing 50 acres, and whereas the said Jno Dorsey has been sued by a certain Nathan Hammond of the City of Annapolis, who obtained judgement, and the said John Dorsey is also considerably indebted to the said Stephen West as well as the said Rachell Hall he assigns all those tracts and also *Mullinix's Chance,* containing 100 acres, purchased of a certain Thos Mullinex for the conveyance of which he has a bond from said Mullineux, and whereas the said John Dorsey is at this time possessed of a Negro boy Phill, aged 7 years; another Negro Jane, about 16 years old; three white servants named Tom, Robert and Mark, also a crop of tobacco in the house upon the lands, being about 5000 lbs. He assigns all of the above. Signed before Wm Hayward.

163-164. Van Swearingen Jr. of Berkeley County, Virginia, recorded deed 19 June 1772, made same day, from Joseph Chapline for £2..10 assigns lot #59 in Town of Sharpsburgh. Van Swearingen agrees to erect a house and other building on the lot.

164-165. Adam Coon recorded deed 18 June 1772, made same day, from Daniel Dulaney for £5 assigns lot in Frederick Town, no. 21, Signed before Thos Price, Benjamin Price.

165-167. Joshua Martin recorded lease 18 June 1772 from Samuel and Bennet Chew in consideration of rents and covnents herein, assigns part of tract called *Chew Farm,* lot #13, for term of 21 years, paying rents. Agrees to build house, plant an apple orchard, and maintain them during the term. Signed Saml Chew, Bennet Chew, Joshua Martin before R. Ghiselin, Wm Stewart. Chas Jones, Saml Beall Junr.

167-168. Samuel Mansell Junr. Recorded bill of sale 18 June 1772. I Samuel Mansell of Anne Arundel County in consideration of the natural love and affection I have for my son, grant Negro girl called Beck, together with her increase. Signed before Eneas Campbell.

168-170. John Weller recorded land commission 21 June 1772 on *Addition to Blacksmith's Lot.* Wm Beatty, Jno Middaugh qualified as commissioners to perpetuate the memory of the bounds of said tract. Deposition of Jacob Weller, 67 years old, a member of the Church known as United Brethren regarding making the survey. Deposition of John Weller, aged about 56 years old, being sworn on the Holy Evangels deposeth that he was present when Thomas Prather laid out the *Addition to Blacksmith's Lot,* and was one of the chain carriers.It began at a branch on the west side of Great Hunton Creek. Deposition of Larrance Creager, about 57 years old, who produced a certificate, being a member of the Church known as the United Brethern, and witnessed that he was present at the survey at *Paysell's Chance,* and was one of the chain carriers, laid out by Nathl Wickham. Deposition of Henry Pysell about 44 years old, sworn, deposeth he was one of the Chain Carriers at making the Survey of *Paysell's Chance*, laid out by Nathl Wickham, the at the 4th course of the

Addition to the Smith's Lot. Deposition of Jacob Weller, being about 67 years old, was also present at Survey of *Paysell's Chance*.

170-171. Zachariah Ellis recorded sale 25 June 1772 from James Wilcoxin for £20..4 sells one feather bed with furniture, one rug, two blankets, a pari of sheets two pillows and bolster, bedstead and bed card, and note of hand of Josias Miles for £11..10 payable 1 Nov. Next ensuing. If redeemed by 1 March 1773, bill of sale void.

171-172. Wm Stevenson recorded deed 22 June 1772 , made 8 April 1772 between Benjamin Paden of Frederick County, farmer, for £250 sells parcel called *Addition to Brooks Discovery on the Rich Lands,* adjacent to Reese Phillip's land, bought of George Buchanan, containing 100 acres, and also 41 acres, part of the aforementioned tract, made over by James Brookes unto Andrew Parks and Abraham Hayter, and 104 acres made over by the same to Benjamin Paden, and 64 acres part of said 104 acres, sold by Benjamin Paden to James Paden. Signed before Jos Wood, Catharine Wood. Jennett the wife of Benjamin Peden released dower before Jos Wood, Wm Blair.

173-174. Christian Kizer recorded deed 22 June 1772 from Benjamin Eastburn for £5 sells part of *Resurvey on Timber Ridge Enlarged,* containing 21 acres. Signed before Thos Price, Chr. Edelin. Jane Eastburn released dower rights.

174-175. Jonathan Fry recorded deed 22 June 1772 from Enoch Fry for £50 sells part of tract called *Longatepaugh,* Signed before Thos Pirce, Chr. Edelin. Receipt, acknowledgment, wife (left blank) of Enoch Fry, examed and released dower rights.

175-177. Henry Leatherman recorded deed 22 June 1772, made 18 June 1772, from John Toms for £100 sells part of *Resurvey on Friendship Dropt,* containing 105 acres. Signed by mark, before Wm Blair, Eneas Campbell. Receipt. Acknowledgment.

177-179. Casper Devilbiss recorded deed 22 June 1772 from Charles Beatty for £702 sells tract, called *Jacob's Pasture,* granted unto Jacob Nathaniel Minsher, metes and bounds given adjoining first line of *Beatty's Garter*, one of the original tracts, containing 492 acres. The second tract called *Resurvey on Beall's Meadow,* metes and bounds given for 165 acres. And The last called *Deer Park,* containing 45 acres. The three tracts contain in the whole 702 acres more or less. Signed C. Beatty before Wm Richey, James Barnes. Martha wife to aforesaid Beatty released dower rights.

179-180. Bartholomew Keefer recorded deed 22 June 1772 from John Cove for £82 sells parcel known as *Resurvey on Locust Neck,* 199 acres. Elizabeth wife of John Cove released dower rights. Witnesses Jos Wood, Wm Blair.

180-182. Peter Krable (Crable) recorded deed 22 June 1772 from Peter Angle (Engle) of Frederick County, cutler, for £90 lot #100 in Frederick Town, 60 ft. by 393 ft. Signed before Thos Price, Ens Campbell. Catharine Angle released doer rights.

182-183. Col. Charles Beatty recorded deed 22 June 1772, made 14 June, from Jacob Miller for £155 sells part of *Deer Park,* on south side of Fishing Creek, containing 45 acres. Signed before Wm Ritchy, James Barnes. Barbara Miller released dower.

183-184. Pearce Lamb recorded deed 22 June 1772, made 18 June from Edward Lamb for £250, part of *Addition to Lambs Choice,* adjacent to Thomas Durbin's land, containing 155 acres. Signed before Jos Wood, Wm Blair. Eleanor, wife of Edward Lamb released dower.

185-186. Henry Leatherman recorded deed 22 June 1772, made 18 June from Conrad Morgan for £3 sells part of *Friendship Dropt,* containing one acre. Signed before Wm Blair, Enes Campbell.

186-188. Martin Funck recorded deed of confirmation 22 June 1772 from Peter French for £230 Pennsylvania, confirms deed made 2 June 1770 on *Resurvey on Dry Bottom,* 133 acres. Signed German Script before Thos Prather, Wm McClurgh. Catharine French released dower.

188-189. Henry Schnebly recorded deed 22 June 1772 from Jonathan Hager for lot #103 in Elizabeth town. Signed before Evan Shelby, Thos Prather.

189-190. Margaret Etenciery of Frederick Co., widow, recorded deed 22 June 1772, made 8 May 1772, from Jane Meek, widow, of Frederick County for £46 Pennsylvania, sells tract *Pleasant Hill,* granted Jane Meek by warrant out of the land office in 1754[43], patented in her name on the East side of Conococheague, on a hill near George Waddle's dwelling, containing 50 acres. Signed by mark before Thos Prather, Evan Shelby.

190-191. Abraham King recorded deed 22 June 1772, made 17 June for 5 shillings, from Martin Whipp for 5 shillings, *Second Resurvey on Good Hill and Corepalse,* two parts, 27 acres and 32 ½ acres. No dower release.

192-193. Benjamin Ogle Jr recorded deed 22 June 1772, made 16 June, from Sarah Henry, heretofore Sarah Ogle, relict and extr. Joseph Ogle late of Frederick County for £100 sells part of *Peace and Plenty,* containing 50 acres. Signed before Thos Prather, Thos Price.

194-195. Jacob Cassell recorded deed 22 June 1772, made 18 June, from Edward Lamb for £85..2 part of *Lambs Choice,* containing 113 acres. Signed before Jos Wood, Wm Blair. Eleanor Lamb released dower rights.

195-197. Hugh Scott recorded deed 22 June 1772, made 13 June, from William Beall for £25 sells tract, *Butler's Gift,* beginning at *Ross's Range,* belonging to John Ross, Esq. on Great Piney Creek, containing 50 acres. Sarah wife of Wm Beall released dower.

197. Enoch Fry recorded receipt 22 June 1772 from Wm Murdock Beall for alienation fine recorded in Liber N:432.

197-198. Conrad Morgan recorded deed 22 June 1772 from Henry Leatherman for £3, tract, *Take Me Now or Not at All,* adjacent to *Friendship Dropt,* for one acre. Signed German script before Wm Blair, Eneas Campbell.

198-200. John Toms recorded deed 22 June 1772, made 18 June, from Henry Leatherman for £100 part of *Maple Bottom,* 20 ½ acres. Signed before Wm Blair, Eneas Campbell

200-201. Christian Koontz recorded deed 22 June 1772, made 9 June, from Marks Harmon for £40 *Nolen Mountain* on Great Hunting Creek, 30 acres. Signed German Script before Jos Wood, Sam Willson.

201-202. Daniel Ragon recorded deed 22 June 1772 , made 9 June, from Mary Biggs, relict of John Biggs, and Joseph Hedges and Sarah Hedges, his wife, late Sarah Biggs, for £50 lot #23 in Frederick Town.

---

[43] Jane Meek, granted 50 acres,, 12 April 1754, survey GS2:230; patent BC4:342.

202-204. Andrew Warman recorded deed 22 June 1772, made 17 June from Simon Meredith, carpenter, for £135 the three following tracts: *Brown's Delight,* 100 yards on the west side of the dwelling house of James Brown Jr., 50 acres; part of *Resurvey on Justice's Delight,* 20 3/4 acres, and part of *Peach Orchard,* 8 ½ acres. Signed before Jos Wood and Charles Jones. Catharine, wife of Samuel Meredith released dower rights.

204-205. Thomas Taylor recorded deed 22 June 1772 from Charles Beatty for £45 sells part of *Resurvey on Mount Pleasant.* Martha Beatty released dower rights.

206-207. John Weller recorded deed 22 June 1772 from Daniel Shultz for 5 shillings, lot #235 in Frederick town. Signed by both.

207. Michael Ott recorded deed 22 June 1772 from William Fream for £33, tract *Good Luck.* Signed before Jos Wood, Wm Blair.

208-209. Charles Beatty recorded deed 22 June 1772, made 17 June, from William Beall for £10 part of *Bealls Meadow,* containing 10 acres. Sarah wife of William Beall released dower.

209-211. Patrick McSherry recorded deed 22 June 1772 from Edward Burk and Wm Burk of Frederick Town, for £120 sells 97 1/4 acres called *Dyer's Mill Forrest,* beginning at 13th line of tract called *Lemon's Range,* Signed by Edward Burk, and Wm Burk by mark before Jos Wood, Geo Clark. Acknowledgment.

211-212. Ulrick Stately recorded deed 22 June 1772, made 17 June, from Saml Chase & Thomas Johnson Jr. of the City of Annapolis, for £45 sells tract called *Colonel,* Signed before D. Hughes. Acknowlegement.

212-213. Joseph Paxton recorded deed 22 June 1772, made 17 June, from William Fream of Frederick County, carpenter, parcel called *Good Luck,* patented to Col. Sam'l Beall and by him conveyed to said Fream. For £75 Signed before Jos Wood, Wm Blair.

213-215. William Willcoxon recorded deed 22 June 1772, made 1 June, from from Rebecca Brooke for £56 sells part of a tract called *Dan,* beginning at the end of the 7th line of part of tract formerly conveyed to William Dent, containing 25 acres more or less. Signed Rebecca Brooke before David Lynn, Zadock Tannehill. Acknowledged before David Lynn, Andrew Heugh.

215-216. Robert Love recorded deed 22 June 1772, made 1 June from Mary Belt of Prince George's County, for £61 sells tract part of *Brook Grove,* metes and bounds given for 80 acres. Signed before David Lynn, Zadock Tannehill.

216-217. Caleb Wilson recorded deed 22 June 1772, made 27 May between Raphael Taney of St. Mary's County, for £50 sells part of a tract called *Resurvey on Brother's Agreement,* on east side of a branch called Joseph Sparke's Branch, descending into Piney Creek, it being the beginning of Jno Stevenson's part of said tract, containing 109 acres more or less. Signed before Thomas Petrie, Edward Mattingly. Receipt. Acknowlegement, Ellen wife of Raphael Taney released dower rights.

217-219. William Chenefield recorded deed 22 June 1772, made 17 June, from George Kissinger for 5 shillings sterling, sells tract called *Great Worth,* part of *Locust Bottom,* containing 43 acres more or less. Elizabeth Kyssinger released dower rights.

219-220. Henry Unger recorded deed 22 June 1772, made 17 June, from William Fream for £16 sells part of tract *Good Luck,* containing 43 acres. Signed before Jno Wood, Wm Blair.

220. John Justice Jr recorded deed 22 June 1772, made 18 June, from John Justice Sr. For £5 sterling, devises tract called *Justice's Delight,* containing 13 acres. Signed by mark before Jos Wood, Wm Blair. Receipt. Mary, wife of Jno Justice Senior released dower.

221-222. Benjamin Gittings recorded deed 22 June 1772, made 1 June 1772, from Rebecca Brooke for £55 sells part of *Dan,* formerly conveyed to Wm Dent, beginning at end of 7th line of said tract, containing 25 acres more or less. Signed before David Lynn, Zadock Tannehill.

223-224. Jno Charlton recorded deed 22 June, made 22 May from Pointon Charlton, for £70 sells tract called *Darling Sale,* devised to him by his father, Jno Charlton, late of Frederick County, deceased, beginning at the 18th line of land called *Darling Sale,* containing 60 acres.

224-226. Isaac Fry recorded deed 22 June 1772, made 18 June, from John Cove for £115 sells tract *Resurvey on Locust Neck,* containing 122 acres. Signed before Wm Blair, Jos Wood. Elizabeth, wife of Jno cove released dower rights.

226-227. John Justice Sr. Recorded deed 22 June 1772, made 18 June, from John Justice Jr. For £5 assigns part of *Justice's Delight,* Signed by mark before Wm Blair, Jos Wood.

227-229. Christian Stover recorded deed 22 June 1772, made 16 June between Philip Knewell of Frederick County, for £95 sells *Resurvey on Shoemaker's Knife,* containing 55 acres. Signed in German Scrip, Johan Philip Knobel, before Chris Edelin, Thos Price.. Receipt. Acknowledgment.

229-230. Abraham Lingenfelter recorded deed 22 June 1772, made 13 June, from William House for £3 sells lot #20 in Sharpsburgh.

230-231. Philip Noland Jr. Of Loudon County, Virginia, recorded deed 22 June 1772, made 25 May, from William Griffith of Loudon County, Virginia, for £30 sells tract called *Partnership,* lying in Frederick County, beginning at a black oak which joins together, on east side of the Main road leading from the Mouth of Monocacy to Frederick Town, Signed before Ens Campbell, Wm Luckett.

231-232.John Wolgamott recorded deed 22 June 1772, made 20 May, from Christian Wise for £360 sells tract called *Water Sink,* containing 62 acres. Signed in German Script before Thos Prather, Basil Prather.

232-234. Charles Ketterows recorded deed 22 June 1772, made 16 June, from Wolfe Space and his present wife, and Christopher Space for £95 sell 50 acres of land, part of *Brother's Agreement,* land surveyed for Christian Hunter. Signed in G.S. by the two men, and by mark by Catherine Space before Jos Wood, Ens Campbell. Catharine wife of Wolfe Space acknowledged dower release.

234-236. Christian Kemp recorded deed 22 June 1772, made 16 June, from Philip Fogel for £300 sells 150 acres, part of 300 acres conveyed to said Ludwick Kemp by Christian Kemp, being part of *Kemps Long Meadow,* Signed German Script. Catharine Fogle released dower rights.

236-237. Henry Fortney recorded deed 22 June 1772, made 18 June, from David Fortney for £6 sells tract called *Resurvey on Limestone Rock,* containing 6 acres. Signed before Thos Price, Benj Price.

237-238. Samuel Wolgamott recorded deed 22 June 1772, made 1 June, from Jacob Eversole for £520 sells parcel called *Helm's Lookout,* adjacent to Christian Eversole's part. Signed before Sam'l Beall Junr., Clement Brooke. Receipt. Acknowledgment. Mary Eversole released dower rights. 239-241. Benjamin Ogle Jr. recorded deed 22 June 1772, made 16 June, from Sarah Henry. Whereas the said Sarah Henry is seized in fee in two tracts, she sells parcels of land called *Ogleton & Kingstonestead* 150 acres, part of *Resurvey on part of Cream* called

Ogleton, and 50 acres, part of *Kingstonestead,* beginning at tract called *Younger Brother,* Signed by mark before Thos Prather, Thos Price. Receipt for £400.

241-242.. George Weaver (Weber) recorded deed 22 June 1772 from George Shiedeler, parcel called *Charming Beauty,* beginning at Spring, near Kitockten Mountain, containing 75 acres. Signed in German Script, before Jos Wood, Charles Jones. Margaret Shideler released dower rights.

242-243. John Shaffer recorded deed 22 June 1772, made 17 June, from Ludwick Harbough for £40 sells tract, part of *Valentine's Garden,* adjacent to *Mason's Folly,* containing 39 acres. Signed German Script, before Thos Price, Benjamin Price, Christenah, wife of Ludwick, released dower.

243-244. Daniel Fortney recorded deed 22 June 1772, made 18 June, between Henry Fortney, for £50, part of *Deer Springs.* 65 acres. Signed before Thos Price, Benj. Price. Receipt.

245-246. Henry Houpman recorded deed 22 June 1772 from Edward Lamb for £50 tract called *Resurvey on Locust Neck,* containing 112 acres. Signed before Jno Coon, C.H. Miers by mark. Eleanor, wife of Edward Lamb released dower rights before Wm Blair, Jno Cove.

246-247. John Rowland recorded deed 22 June 1772 from Michael Haince of Baltimore County, for £122 sells tract called *Pleasant Springs,* adjacent to *Good Spring,* Signed in German Script before Wm Harris, James Forbes. The wife of Michael Haines (name left blank) examined and released dower rights.

248-249. Andrew Kessler, cordwainer, recorded deed 22 June 1772 from James Beall and Elizabeth his wife, late called Elizabeth Pooly, widow of Mathias Pooly, planter, for £50 sells part of tract called *Mistaken Rival,* formerly the estate of the siad Mathias Pooly deceased, and by his will bequeath unto Elizabeth Pooly, her heirs and assigns, containing 50 acres. Signed by James Beall, Elizabeth Beall by mark before Thos Price, James Town Rigby.

249-251. John Snavely recorded deed 22 June 1772, made 17 June from Nicholas Sam, for 5 shillings, sterling, assigns tract called *The Addition to Rosburies Delight,* beginning at a bounded black oak on the ridge on the east side of Tonoloway Creek, near half a mile from James Dawson's house. On the southwest side thereof, containing 30 acres. Signed before Thos Brice, Benjamin Rice.

251-252. William Chanefield recorded deed 22 June 1772, made 17 June, from George Kyssinger for £200 assigns parcel called *Little Worth,* containing 100 acres. Signed before Jos Wood, Wm Blair. Elizabeth Kyssinger released dower rights.

252-254. George Yose recorded deed 25 June 1772, made 22 May from William Johnson. Whereas a tract of land called *Small Meadow,* was originally granted to Christopher Michael and from him conveyed to Wm Johnston by deed recorded in liber I 1315 & 1316, as also one other tract called *Goose Bill,* originally granted a certain Nicholas Fink and by him conveyed to Wm Johnson, in Liber G folio 1233 & 1234; now this indenture witnesseth that Wm Johnson for £155 conveys unto George Youse all those tracts, standing on a draught of Kittocktin Creek, containing 100 acres, and 26 acres of land more or less, assigned to Geo Yose. Signed by mark before Thos Johnson, Thos Brice. Elizabeth wife to Wm Johnson released dower rights.

254-256. Thomas Robey recorded lease 3 July 1772, made 24 May, from Saml Chew and Bennett Chew of Anne Arundel County, (Chews Farm) lot #18, containing 100 acres. Signed by all parties.

256-258. Sylvanus Porter recorded lease 3 July 1772 from Saml Chew and Bennett Chew of Anne Arundel County, for rents and covenents herein, a tract, part of Chews Farm, Lot #29, containing 100 acres, for term of 21 years. Signed by all parties before R. Ghiselin and Wm Stewart.

258-260. Peter Barnes recorded lease 3 July 1772 from Saml Chew and Bennett Chew of Anne Arundel County, for rents and covenents herein, a tract, part of Chews Farm, Lot #27, containing 100 acres, for term of 21 years. Signed by all parties before R. Ghiselin and Wm Stewart.

260-262. Clement Howard recorded lease 3 July 1772 from Saml Chew and Bennett Chew of Anne Arundel County, for rents and covenents herein, a tract, part of Chews Farm, Lot #25, containing 100 acres, for term of 21 years. Signed by all parties before R. Ghiselin and Wm Stewart.

262-264. Peter Roby recorded lease 3 July 1772 from Saml Chew and Bennett Chew of Anne Arundel County, for rents and covenents herein, a tract, part of Chews Farm, Lot #7, containing 100 acres, for term of 21 years. Signed by all parties before R. Ghiselin and Wm Stewart.

264-266. Emanuel Braulier recorded deed 8 July 1882 from Jacob Rine and Barbary his wife, and Frederick Naugle and Mary his wife, all of Frederick County. For £40 they sell tract called *Wife's Fancy,* standing at the end of a line from John Wilson's bound tree, containing 51 acres more or less. Signed by the four grantees before Jos Wood, Thos Price.

267-268. Joseph Wood Jr. Recorded deed 8 July 1772 from Michael Dutteror for £29 sells tract part of *Spring Plains,* Signed by mark, before Jos Wood, Thos Price. Susanna Dotter release dower rights.

268-269. Charles Carroll Jun. of Prince George's County, recorded deed 8 July 1772 from Robert Beall (son of James) of Frederick County, for £269..10 sells tract called *Second Addition to Hazard,* Robert Beall signed before David Lynn, Abraham Davenport.

269-271. Jacob Linebaugh recorded deed 8 July 1772, made 18 June 1772, from Thomas Brooke for £140 Pennsylvania, tract of land called *German Town,* containing 102 acres. Another tract, *Imperatous Liberatus,* beginning at 11th line of tract called *Vine Garden,* in the possession of a certain Ludowick Butts, on Broad Run, a draught of Great Hunting Creek, containing 20 acres moe or less; signed before Chs Jones, Wm Blair.

271-272. George Adam Ridenhour recorded deed 8 July 1772 from Thomas Brooke for £10 *All That I can Get,* beginning at tract called *Copeland,* granted to Peter Copeland, also the beginning tree of *Jerusalem,* belonging to Peter Frederick Willhite.

272-273. Michael Thomas Sr. recorded deed 8 July 1772 from Peter Hill for £150 for *Peter's Good Luck,* a part of the *Resurvey on Stoney Glade,* 100 acres. Catharine Hill released dower rights.

273-274. Michael Thomas recorded deed 8 July 1772 from Jacob Bruner for £90 assigns *Bruner's Lot,* at the end of the second line of *Resurvey on Stoney Glade,* signed in German script. Margaret Bruner released dower rights.

275. Jacob Linebaugh recorded deed 8 July 1772 from Jacob Weller for £2 tract called *Taylor's Lot,* 4 acres. Margaret Weller released dower rights.

276. Thomas Beall recorded deed of gift 16 July 1772 from George Beall for love, gratitude and affection to son, tract called *Beall's Chance,* adjacent to *Nelson's Folly,* taken up by Arthur Nelson.

276-277. John Hardy recorded lease 11 July 1772 from Charles Carroll Jr. of Prince George's County, part of *Aix La Chappelle*, for 23 years, for rents and covenents herein, to build frame dwelling, plant 100 apple trees.

277-278. Edmund Jennings recorded deed 26 July 1772 from Daniel Carroll for £113, tract called *Henry and Mary*, on Middle Seneca Creek, 110 acres, and parcel called *Dorsey's Plains*, granted William Wofford, beginning at Cattail Branch, off of Middle Seneca, 10 acres. Witnesses Daniel Hughes, Sarah Hughes.

279, 280. Conrad Nicholdemas recorded deed 23 July 1772 from Peter Berghman for £520 , two tracts on Antietam, the first called *Peter's Part*, at end of *Resurvey on the Good*, also the last line of *Nelson's Folly*, where Robert Turner now lives, 100 acres. The second tract called *Barkman's Choice*, beginning at tract called *Charlemount Pleasant*, containing 49 3/4 acres. Signed in German Script, Peter Berghman, before Sam'l Beall Jr., David Meek. Elizabeth, wife of Peter Barkman, released dower rights. Alienation fine paid.

281-282. Daniel of St. Thos Jenifer recorded deed 24 July 1772, made 18 May 1772 from William Reynolds, both of Annapolis for £100 tract called *Resurvey on Mitchell's Range*, signed before Wm Steuart, Robt Condon.

282-283. Jacob Evey (Avey) recorded deed 25 July 1772 from George Williams for £220, part of tract called *Rogues Harbour*, beginning at a tract called *Captain John's Bottom*, taken up by Adam Sherill[44], tract containing 49 ½ acres. Signed by mark, before Thomas Prather, Jenny Prather. Elizabeth wife of George Williams released dower rights.

284-285. [279a. Duplicate] Jacob Smith recorded deed 29 July 1772 from Edward Grimes for £56 two tracts, the first *Betty's Good Will*, at the foot of Shanendore Mountain, near the wagon road that goes from Feagens Ferry to Monocacy Town, containing 50 acres. Also tract called *Grime's Purchase*, part of the *Resurvey on Mend All*, containing 50 acres. [this page 279a, also 284, inserted between two pages of deed above on the microfilm]. Signed before Jon Shelby, Jarvis Hougham. Anne Grime released dower rights.

285-286. Jos. & Robt Wood recorded deed 11 August 1772 from Nathaniel Wickham, for £5 sterling, tract *Wickham's Discovery*, beginning at a tract called *Buck Range*, containing 81 acres.. [pg. 286 missing from microfilm & on-line versions]. Signed by Nathaniel Wickham. Sarah Wickham released dower.

286-287. Jacob Good recorded bill of sale 13 Aug. 1772 from George Clarke of Taney Town, for £4 sells milch cow, bed stead, blankets, black trunk, other items. 287. George Clarke acknowledged bill of sale.

287-288. Peter Fine recorded release 13 August 1772 from William Albough, who obtained judgment in Frederick County Court in 1769 for £29... and attached to tract called *Hobson's Choice*, containing 150 acres. Signs release in consideration of payment before Christopher Edelin, Thomas Price.

---

[44] Patented 20 Oct 1740 for 100 acres by Adam Sherrill, Prince George's County, recorded in E15/555;E16/302. Reference checked because of difficulty reading name in deed.

288-289. Daniel Culp recorded power of attorney 19 Aug 1772 from James Mendenhall and Agnes Mendallhall his wife, of Barkley County, Virginia, to recover debts due. Signed before Stephen Thatcher, Martha Woodenhall.

289-290. Thos Sprigg Wootton recorded deed 20 Aug. 1772 from James Stimpson for £150, parcels, part of *Exchange and New Exchange,* beginning at branch that runs into Watts Branch, 200 acres; also another part of same tract, containing 100 acres; and part of tract called *Cuckold's Delight,* 24 acres. Signed by mark before David Lynn, Ans Campbell.

290-291. Rev. James Hunt recorded deed of trust 20 August 1772 from Col. George Beall, considering that no provisions made for Presbyterian Society and members of the Church of Scotland, whereon to build a church and bury their dead, for 10 shillings, grants lot on tract called *Conjurer's Disappointment.* Signed George Beall.

291-293. James Stympson recorded deed 20 August 1772 from Richard Keene of Prince George's County, for £140 parcels, part of *Exchange and New Exchange,* on part of Watts Branch, 200 acres.

293-294. Samuel Hughes recorded deed 20 Aug. 1772 from Daniel Hughes for 5 shillings, *Resurvey on Chester,* 388 acres. Signed before Thomas Prather, Evan Shelby.

294 Daniel Hughes recorded deed 20 Aug. 1772 from Samuel Hughes, same tract as above.

294-295. Sarah Barnes recorded deed of gift 20 Aug 1772 from Samuel Hobbs, son of William, for the natural love and affection he has for Sarah and for 5 shillings, one Negro boy named Tom to Sarah and the lawful heirs of her body, but if at the decease of said Sarah Barnes, there are no heirs, then the slave is to be returned to Samuel Hobbs, as if this sale never occurred.

295-296. Henry Gaither recorded deed 20 Aug. 1772 from Benjamin Clary for £20, part of a tract called *Moab,* on draught of Linganore. Signed before Thomas Price, Richard Gassaway.

297-298. Daniel Miller recorded deed 19 Aug. 1772 from James Hook, part of *Resurvey on Anchor and Hope,* includes, land and mills, etc. Signed before Ans Campbell, John Maynard.

298-300. Benoni Dawson recorded 20 Aug. 1772, made 20 Aug. 1772 between William Littlefield of FC, for 110 pcm, sells tract included within 2nd *Resurvey on William and John,* beginning at a tract of land called *Mother's Delight,* containing 110 acres. Signed Willm Littlefield. Receipt. Ack., Rebecca Littlefield released dower before David Lynn, Thos Sprigg Wootton.

300-302. Francis Deakins and William Deakins Jr. recorded deed 20 Aug. 1772 from Zachariah White for £512 parcel called *Wellfare,* beginning at a bound white oak on north side of Little Monocacy, 7 acres of land. Also part of *Resurvey on Buck Field,* containing 6 acres. Signed before Andrew Heugh, Charles Jones. Mary White released dower rights.

302-304. Richard Wootton of PGC, recorded 20 August 1772 made 19 Aug. 1772, between William Littlefield of FC, for 400 pcm MD, sells tract part of *Second Addition to William and John,* beginning at a black oak on west side of a branch about 40 ft. from said branch, and about 40 yards below head of said branch that falls into Seneca, running thence to the bounded tree of a tract of land of Ninian Beall's, containing 437 acres more or less, with all houses, outhouses, buildings, gardens, orchards, fences, water courses, and improvements etc., signed Willm Littlefiled, before David Lynn. Receipt. Rebecca Littlefield released dower.

304-305. Yost Blickerstaffer recorded deed 30 Aug. 1772 from Abigail Ferguson for 5 shillings, assigns her dower right in tract called *DeButt's Hunting Lodge*[45], conveyed by a certain Abigail Armitt, daughter of Abigail Ferguson, by her for her husband. Signed before Thomas Prather, Evan Shelby.

305-306. John Hilton recorded lease 25 Aug. 1772 from Samuel Plummer in consideration of covenants hereafter, assigns part of *Plummer's Delight,* for term of 29 years to him and heirs of his body, to pay £20 yearly and to maintain buildings. Signed by both parties before David Lynn, T. Sprigg Wootton.

307-309. Nicholas Vinnamon recorded land commission issued to Nathaniel Newbitt, Richard Prather, Devall Ankenny and George Gillespie, to perpetuate the bounds of tract. Signed by Thos Sprigg, clerk, 5 Sept. 1771. Deposition of Col. Thomas Prather aged 70 years, or thereabouts, about 25 or 26 years ago, he was brought to bound black oak stump about 12 to 15 ft. high by Evan Shelby Sr., that it was the bound tree of tract of land called *Mouldy Pine,* stump has decayed away, and limestone put in the place where it stood. Deposition of Captain Evan Shelby about 48 years old, states about 30 years ago , regarding tract called *Mouldy Pine,* in company with Joseph Chapline and Evan Shelby his father. 309. Affirmation of Jacob Gripe Junior 31 years old, deposeth that 10 or 11 years ago, he was brought to place where bounded tree stood, where parcel of limestone, as a chain carrier, to the beginning of a certain Conrad Hogmire's land, who ran the lines of said land, and it was the same place. Signed in German Script by Jacob Greib.

309-310. James Dick of Anne Arundel County, recorded deed 22 Aug. 1772 from Arthur Nelson for 5 shillings, part of *Exchange and New Exchange,* withed before Thomas Johnson Junr., C. Beatty.

310-312. Andrew Stous, recorded deed 25 August 1772 from Henry Unger for £40, part of *Addition to Brooke's Discovery on the Rich Lands,* containing 100 acres. Signed by mark before Jos Wood, Wm Blair. Catherine Unger, released dower rights.

312-314. Daniel Delozier recorded deed 25 Aug. 1772 from George Church for £180, for *Resurvey on Antietam Level,* on east side of Antietam Creek, near Cartlidge's Old Road, containing 109 acres. Signed in German Script, Gorg Kirg, Jane his wife released dower.

314-315. Sam'l Hocker recorded 1 Sept. 1772. Made 21 Aug. 1772 between Wm Littlefield of FC, for 50 pcm MD, sells a tract called the Second Resurvey of *William and John,* beginning at end of 125 pc. on the 4th line of the said Resurvey, running M&B until it intersects Benoni Dawson's part of the said land, then with Dawson's part to the beginning. Also another part of the said Resurvey, beginning at the beginning of the 114th line of said land, to the beginning. Also part of the first Resurvey beginning at the end of 33rd line of the said land. Containing 209 acres more or less. Signed Wm Littlefield. Rebecca Littlefield released dower.

315-317. William Purdy recorded deed 25 August 1772 from Joseph Ridgeway of Frederick County, Commonwealth of Virginia, for £100 sells part of tract called *William and Elizabeth,* above spring that runs into Dumpling Creek on north side of a fork of Bennett's Creek, for 100 acres. Signed Jos Wood, William Blair.

---

[45] Robert DeButts patented tract 16 August 1742, Prince George's County, E16/518; LGE/78. Peter Wilson Coldham, *Settlers of Maryland 1731-1750,* p. 60. Word "Lodge" illegible in this deed.

317-318. George Coller recorded deed 25 Aug. 1772 from Henry Hall, son and heir of Henry Hall, deceased of Anne Arundel, County, for 5 shillings, assigns part of *Resurvey on Nicholas Mistake,* containing 104 acres by estimation.

318-319. Peter Fleurgate recorded deed 23 Aug. 1772 from Henry Hall son and heir of Henry Hall, deceased of Anne Arundel, County, for 5 shillings, assigns part of *Resurvey on Nicholas Mistake,* containing 290 acres by estimation.

319-320 John Hoover recorded deed 25 Aug. 1772 from Henry Hall son and heir of Henry Hall, deceased of Anne Arundel, County, for 5 shillings, assigns the remaining part of *Resurvey on Nicholas Mistake.*

320-321. Daniel McCormick recorded deed 25 Aug 1772 from George Gump of York County, Pennsylvania, for £105 assigns tract called *Gump's Addition,* containing 165 acres. Sarah Gump released dower right.

321-323. Joseph Hagan recorded deed 25 August 1772 from Thomas Burgee (or Burgess), tract called *Flip N Easy,* conveyed Thomas Burgess by Wm Duvall, reference in Anne Arundel County, for £139, beginning at bounded tree a tract called *Joseph's Adventure,* signed by mark before David Lynn, T. Sprigg Wootton. Eleanor, wife to said Thomas Burgeys released dower rights.

323-324. John Harmon Yost recorded deed 25 August 1772 from Mathias Brandenburg for £7 one lot of land in Middletown, #4, signed before Sam'l Beall Junr., Thos Price. Esther Brandenburg released dower rights.

324-325. Peter Erb Jr. Recorded deed 25 August 1772 from Thomas Estep Sr. For £36 sells tract called *Empty Bottle,* near Little Bear Branch for 50 acres. Mary the wife of Thos Estep released dower rights.

325-326. Jno Haas recorded deed 25 August 1772 from Matthias Nead for £67..10, lot #270 in Frederick Town. Catharine Need released dower rights.

326-327. John Maynard recorded deed 25 Aug. 1772 from Henry Gaither for £85 sells interest in tract called *Hammond's Strife,* on draught of Little Pipe Creek, at end of 6th line of original, patented to John Hammond containing 108 acres. Signed before Ans Campbell, Henry Green.

327-328. Jeremiah Ducker recorded deed 25 Aug. 1772 Christopher Cunningham possessed of part of a tract called *Snowden's Manor Enlarged,* adjacent to tract sold Samuel Godman, containing 150 acres. Signed by mark before David Lynn, James Brooke. Receipt for £305. Mary Cunningham released dower rights.

328-329. Robert Croan recorded deed 28 Aug. 1772 from William Frame (Fream), carpenter, of York County, Pennsylvania, for £100, assigns tract called *Good Luck,* conveyed by Col. Samuel Beall to the said William Fream, containing 140 acres. Signed before Jos Wood, Wm Blair.

329-330. James Leech recorded deed 25 August 1772 from Anthony Sell Jr., of York County, Pennsylvania for £151..10, 131 ½ acres of land called *The Exchange,* beginning at 11th line, adjacent to John Patterson's land, to Daniel Long's land, to John Paxton's land. Signed in German Script, before Jos Wood, Wm Blair. Catharine, wife of Anthony Sell released dower rights.

330-331. John Rineberger recorded deed 25 Aug. 1772 from Jacob Coonce for £41, lot #35 in Taney Town, on the main road to York Town.

331-332. George Jantz recorded deed 25 Aug. 1772 from George Horst of Loudon County, Virginia, for £73 sells lot #135 in Frederick Town, signed in German Script, Johannes Gorg Horsh, before Samuel Beall Jr., and Evan Shelby. Cathrine Hors released dower rights.

332-333. Philip Treigh [Truck ?] recorded deed 25 Aug. 1772 from Henry Unger, for £18..18 part of *Brooke's Discovery on the Rich Lands,* containing 32 ½ acres. Signed by mark. Catharine Unger released dower rights.

333-334. Rudolph Rohr recorded deed 25 Aug. 1772 from Henry Brunner for £20, one fourth part of lot #82 in Frederick Town. Signed in German Script. Magdalena wife of Henry Bruner, released dower rights.

334-335. Adam Bean recorded deed 20 August 1772 from Frederick Whitman for £150 sells tract *Whiteman's Loss,* beginning at *Hedge's Delight,* Signed in German script before Thomas Price, Evan Shelby. Catherine wife of Frederick Whitman released dower.

335-336. Joseph Hurs recorded deed 25 August 1772 from Levi Mills, heir of Thomas Mills, late of said county, deceased, for £50 assigns tract called *Lean's Fields*[46], 35 acres; all that part called *Cutly (or Costly),* 13 acres of land. Signed before Thomas Prather, Basil Prather. Elizabeth Mills, wife of Levi Mills released dower.

336-337. Ezekial Cox recorded deed 25 Aug. 1772 from William Harrison for £5 sells tract called *Maidenhead,* 136 acres. Signed before Thomas Price, Ans Campbell.

337-338. Hance Wendle Rine recorded deed 25 Aug. 1772 from Thomas Fisher of York County, Pennsylvania, for £200, tract called *Brother's Agreement,* 100 acres. Signed before Jos Wood, Wm Blair. Eve Fisher released dower.

338-340. Peter Baker recorded deed 25 Aug. 1772 from Jno MacClaland and Saml Irwin and Elizabeth Irwin his wife, heirs to the estate of Hugh MacClayland, late of Frederick County, deceased, for £509 sells tracts called *Back Meadow.* Jane MacClayland, widow of Hugh, and Martha MacClayland released dower rights before Thomas Prather, Samuel Beall.

340-341. Jonathan Burch of Prince George's County recorded deed 25 August 1772 from Joseph Harris Senior for £75 assigns parcel containing 134 1/4 acres. Signed before William Luckett, Aeneas Campbell. Elizabeth Harris released dower rights.

342. Henry Green recorded deed 25 Aug. 1772 from Henry Gaither for £100 sells all his interest in part of tract called *Hammond's Strife,* containing 100 acres.

343-344. Ludwig Kesseburg recorded deed 25 August 1772 from George Martin for £150 for two parts of a tract called *The Company,* containing 225 acres. Signed in German Script, before Thos Price, Wm Richey. Catherine Martin released dower.

344-345. Daniel Swigert recorded deed 25 August 1772 from Christian Leatherman, for £9..15 sells tract called *Shady Grove,* signed in German Script before Jos Wood, Wm Blair. Barbara Leatherman released dower rights.

---

[46] Thomas Mills patented *Lean's Fields,* 22 May 1765 for 233 acres in Frederick County. BC26/376; BC27/270. He patentented *Costly,* 20 May 1767 for 35 acres, Frederick County, BC36/175; BC40/141. Peter Wilson Coldham, *Settlers of Maryland, 1751-1765,* and *Settler's of Maryland 1766-1783.*

345-346. Richard Stevens recorded deed 25 June 1772 from William Young for £7 sells tract called *Poplar Spring,* containing 29 acres. Signed by mark before Evan Shelby, Thomas Schley. Juliana Young released dower rights.

346-347. John Gist recorded deed 25 July 1772 from Thomas Estep for £30 sells tract called *Rock Spring,* adjacent to tracts called *Lime Pitt,* and *Tom and Wills Valley and Hills,* signed by mark before Thos Price, Ens Campbell. Mary Estep his wife released dower rights.

347-348. Christian Lafevre recorded deed 25 Aug. 1772 from Peter Brunner for £50 sells part of tract called *High Germany,* containing 20 acres. Signed before Thos Price, Evan Shelby. Catherine Bruner released dower rights.

348-349. Lawrence Brengle recrded deed 25 August 1772 from Michael Raymer for £32..5 part of *Park Meadow.* Signed in German Script before David Lynn, Charles Jones. Charlotte Raymer released dower rights.

349-350. George Snider recorded deed 25 August 1772 from Charles Shell for £100, sells lot in Frederick Town, conveyed by Casper Myer. Signed before Joseph Wood, Josia Darby. Rebecca Shell released dower rights.

350-351. Leonard Shown recorded deed 25 Aug. 1772 from Patrick Hines (Hynes) for £2..3..2 and £5..8.. Confirms to him 13 ½ acres, part of *Resurvey on Hibernia,* signed by mark before Thomas Price, Jacob Miller. Mary wife of Patrick released dower rights.

351-352. Jno Middagh recorded deed 25 August 1772, made 7 August 1772 between James Barnes for £12, lot in Addition to Georgetown, made over to him by Beatty and Hawkins, signed before Thomas Price. Receipt, acknowledgment.

352-352a-353. Lewis Keefer recorded deed 24 Aug. 1772 from Abraham Hill for [sum illegible, paper appears to be torn] part of tract called *Frenchman's Purchase,* [dower release also illegible, on part of paper that seems to be covered with mending paper, not visible on microfilm].

353-354. Henry Unger recorded deed 25 August 1772 from Lewis Kiver, part of *Frenchman's Purchase,* signed in German Script, Ludwig Keefer, Margaret wife of Lewis released doer rights. Acknowledged before Jos Wood, Wm Blair.

354-355. George Castle recorded deed 25 Aug. 1772 from Frederick Garrison for £2..5 sells and assigns tract in Frederick County, called *Little Friendship,* adjacent to Muddy Spring, on a draught of Kitocktin Creek, taken up by Jno Johnson, containing 50 acres more or less. Signed by mark before Wm Blair, Jos Wood.

355-356. Mareen Duvall recorded deed 23 August 1772 from Dennis Madden for £250 two tracts beginning at east line of *Joseph's Park* and the *Hermitage,* containing 200 acres.. Signed by mark before Charles Jones, Andrew Heugh. Anastacy Madden, wife of Dennis Madden released dower rights.

356-357. John Gripe recorded deed 25 Aug. 1772 from Andrew Blair for £105 assigns part of tract called *Resurvey on the Mountain of Wales,* adjacent to tract of land called *Spring Hill* containing 200 acres. Signed before Thos Prather, Evan Shelby. Wm M. Beall received alienation fine.

357-359. Patrick Beall recorded deed 27 Aug. 1772 from Walter Evans of Prince George's County, for £300 sells part of *Addition to the Rock of Dumbarton,* Signed before Charles Jones, Andrew Heugh. Elizabeth, wife of Walter Evans examined apart released dower rights.

359. Mary White recorded deed 24 Aug 1772 from Zachariah White, in consideration of the natural love and affection thjat I bear unto my daughter Mary White, and other good causes, give to her, one lot in the Addition to Georgetown, #223, also one Negro woman, Dinah and her increase, one horse and saddle, cow and calf, ewes and lambs, four pigs; and in case of the death of my daughter Mary, before she attains 21 years or has issue lawfully begotton, then I gave those items to my daughter Eleanor; provided nonetheless that they shall not possess them until after my own death and the death of my wife Mary. Signed Zachariah White before Andrew Heugh, Charles Jones.

359-360. Robert Beall White recorded deed 24 Aug 1772 from Zachariah White, for natural love and affection for my beloved son, grant my dwelling plantaion, being the following parcels of land, part of *Groves Hunting Quarter,* containing 36 acres of land; part of *Good Luck*, containing 4 1/4 acres; part of *Resurvey on Partnership*, and part of *Fletchalls Good Will*, containing 8 acres; the whole containing 130 acres of land;; also a feather bed and furniutre, horse, and cow and calf, lamb, two ewes, and pigs. Items to go to my son Zachariah White, should Robert not attain 21 years, and gifts not to take place until after my death and the death of my wife Mary. Signed before Charles Jones, Andrew Heugh.

360-361. Alexander Thomas Hawkins of Prince George's County, recorded assignment of lease 3 Sept 1772 from Nicholas Hook. Whereas by indenture of 15 May 1748 made between the said Alexander Thos Hawkins and a certain Andrew Roderock of Frederick County, for consideration therein did let and assign part of tract called *Hawkins Merry Peep a Day,* lying in said county and on the division line of said Alexander Thos Hawkins and Jno Stone Hawkins land, adjacent to the second line of Peter Lodge's part of said land, containing 200 acres more or less, leased to the said Andrew Roderick, Christina Roderick, wife of the said Andrew and Jno Roderick son of Andrew and Christiana, for rents and covenants therein. Whereras the said Andrew Roderick by indenture 1 March 1770 did for consideration therein, assign lease to the said Nicholas Hook. Lease agreement signed in German Script by Nicholas Hook before Thos Price, Aens Campbell.

361-362. Wm Murdock Beall recorded bill of sale 7 Sept. 1772 from John Madden Jr. For £30 assigns two Negroes, woman Dinah about 18 years of age, and a girl named Rachel about 2 years of age, the property of said John Madden, which property came to him by his wife; which bill of sale is to be void and of no effect if sum paid with interest by 1st August next. Signed John Madden before Michel Shyrock, Thos Price.

362-363. Jno Berry, Leonard Wayman, both of Frederick County, and James White of Prince George's County, Doctor Anthony Yeldall of Philadelphia, Pennsylvania recorded articles of agreement 2 Sep 1772. Witnesseth that John Barry has a tract of land in Frederick County called *Babcock,* containing 31 acres, whereon it is supposed that there is a lead or copper mine, it is agreed that the other parties will secure 108 acres to be laid off as the said John Barry shall direct, and to be patents in all of the partners names, and that each partner may have an equal right to the said 109 acres as well as the said 31 acres of land, as it is not convenient for the said Jno Barry to advance any cash for finding tools or provisions for opening the mine; various agreements to share profits. Signed in the presence of James Smith, Richard Richard and Thos Fletcher.

363-365. Abraham Barnes of St. Mary's County, recorded deed 12 Sept. 1772 from Evan Shelby. Whereas a certain Thomas Jennings of Annapolis, in November 1771, conveyed to Abraham Barnes, certain tracts in Frederick County, called *Maiden's Choice,* containing 318 acres and *Shelby's Misfortune,* containing 250 acres; and *Hanover* 1010 acres; also part of *Kindness* containing 475 acres and whereas a certain Stephen West of Prince George's County in November 1771, onveyed to Abraham Barnes, part of *Mountain of Wales*, which was formerly the property of Evan Shelby, he conveys parts not previously conveyed, originally containing 9860 acres; but parts have been conveyed to Jacob Gripe, David Jones Junior, Isaac Baker, Jacob Levi, Joseph Pritchard, Andrew Blair, Peter Jones, Dewalt Ankeny, Peter Parsley, Thomas Bowles, Samuel Chase, Lancelot Jacques, and Thomas Junior [sic], Joseph Fue, George Gelespie, David Shelby and Jacob Veryfield, and part to Stephen West containing by estimation 1260 acres; the intent of the parties. Signed by Evan Shelby before Thomas Prather, Thomas Price. Letita Shelby released dower rights.

365-368. Jacob Richards recorded lease and release 13 Sep. 1772 from Alexander Thomas Hawkins of Prince George's county, for rents and considerations, assigns part of *Hawkins Merry Peep a Day*, containing 200 acres more or less. Signed in the presence of Wm Leek Weems, John Baynes.

368-369. Henry Unsell recorded bill of sale 16 Sep 1772 from Henry Wall for £102, sells one wagon, four horses gears, 5 cows, one heifer, 3 sheep, one sow, 5 pigs, 30 bushels of wheat, and all household good, furniture, and a note for £38 due from George Hessinger on account. Signed in German Script, Henrich Wahl before John Stull, Thomas Welsh. Acknowledgement.

369. Abraham Laken recorded deed of confirmation 16 Sept. 1772 from Fielder Gantt, iron master, for part of *Fielderia Manor,* signed both parties before Sam Jones Rigby.

370-371. Robert White Flemming recorded deed 17 Sept. 1772 from Zachariah White for £12, lot in Georgetown. Mary White released dower. Acknowledged before Andrew Heugh, Charles Jones.

371-372. Robert White Flemming recorded deed 17 Sept. 1772 from Zachariah White for £5 tract called *Hobson's Choice,* on branch called Captain John, bounded in deed from Doctor James Douell to Zachariah White, 7 ½ acres. Receipt, acknowledgment, same witnesses. Mary White released dower.

372-374. James White recorded deed 17 Sep 1772 from Zachariah White for part of *Good luck,* beginning at south line of Ninian Mocabee's part of said land, containing 48 acres; also part of tract called *Addition to Fellowship,* a conveyance from Hugh Tomlinson to Dr. David Ross, James White and Zachariah Whtie, beginning at first line, containing 50 acres. Signed before same witnesses. Mary Whtie released dower rights.

374-375. Michael Graff recorded deed 17 Sep 1772 from Thadeus Beall for lot #39 in Georgetown. Signed before David Lynn, William Deakins Jr. Receipt, acknowledgment. Alienation fine paid to Wm Murdoch Beall.

375-377. Zachariah White recorded deed 17 Sept. 1772 from Edmond Turner of Prince George's County, for £9 *Fletchalls Good Will,* containing 80 acres. Signed before Charles Jones, Andrew Heugh. Catherine Turner released dower rights.

377-378. John Mummert recorded deed 17 Sept. 1772 from James Trail of Amherst County, Virginia for £50 tract called *Trail's Choice,* at first line of tract called *Good Will,* surveyed for David

Trail on the south side of Seneca Creek, containing 50 acres. Signed by mark before Wm Luckett, Aeneas Campbell.

378-380. Casper (Gasper) Swing recorded deed 17 Sept. 1772 from Zachariah Chaney for £20 Tract called *Chaney's Choice,* beginning at bound hickory, on a hill, 1/4 mile from Chaney's dwelling house, containing 27 acres. Signed by mark before Evan Shelby, John Stull. Ann Chaney released dower rights.

380-382. David Crawford of Prince George's county recorded deed 17 Sept 1772 from John West, son of John, for £337 made 17 August for part of tract called *The Joseph,* 48 acres; also part of *Resurvey on Arpos,* 814 acres, exclusive of 1 acre conveyed to Jacob Fouts, and also part of *Addition to Rays Town,* 20 3/4 acres. Signed John West Junior before Andrew Heugh, Charles Jones. Rachel West, wife of said John released dower rights.

382-383. Stephen Wood recorded lease 26 Sept. 1772 from Elisha Williams for rents and considerations herein, tract called *Friends Advise,* containing 100 acres, for 14 years. Signed Elisha Williams, before Thomas Price, Christian Edlen.

383-384. Charles Jones, son of John, Recorded assignment of lease 29 Sep. 1772 from John Cooper administrator of Mary Ann Cooper, deceased, lease given by a certain Alexander Magruder to Mary Ann Cooper 14 May 1760 for consideration of her being married to my father. Signed John Cooper before Robert Peter, Luke Wheeler.

384-385. Jacob Schley recorded deed 28 September 1772 from Jacob Ropp for £90 for lot #6 on road leading from Frederick to Conococheague. Signed in German Script. Margaret Rople [sic ?] released dower rights.

385-387. Jacob Stower recorded deed 17 Sept 1772 from James White, for several parts of *Resurvey on Stulls Forest,* metes and bounds given, 70 acres, and 100 acres and others. Signed before Evan Shelby, John Stull. Sarah White released dower rights.

387-388. Bartholomew Boocher recorded deed 1 Oct. 1772 from Daniel Dulaney, made 17 June 1772, for £120, tract called *Nettle,* containing 50 acres. Signed before Thos Prather, Aeneas Campbell.

388-389. Robt Peter and Anthony Holmead recorded deed 23 Jany 1772 from Samuel Beall Jr. For £125, sells tract called *Widow's Mite,* on north side of Rock Creek, laid out for 11 acres. Signed before Thos Prather, Evan Shelby. Eleanor Beall released dower rights.

389-390. Thomas Davis recorded deed 13 Oct. 1772 from Elizabeth Davis in consideration of the love and affection for my son Thomas Davis assign all my goods, wares, household stuff, after my death, provided nevertheless, if I should have one or more children of my body, then goods to be equally divided. Signed Elizabeth Davis before Sarah Howard, Elizabeth Howard. Acknowledged before David Lynn.

390-391. Balser Heck of Frederick Town, baker, recorded deed 9 Oct 1772 from Balser Bough of Frederick Town, taylor, for £250 half part of lot #29, adjoins Doctor Adam Baker. Signed before Thos Price, Jos Wood. Receipt for current money, Pennsylvania. Rosanna wife of Balser Bough released dower rights. Alienation fine paid Wm M Beall.

392-393. William Deakins Jr. Recorded deed 9 Oct 1772 from John West son of John for £335..10 assigns part of *The Joseph,* beginning at bound tree on north side of the Muddy Branch of Potomack, near the beginning of tract, containing 135 acres. Mentions David Crawford's interest. Signed by John West Junr. before Charles Jones, Andrew Heugh. Rachel West released dower rights.

393-394. Solomon Ellis recorded deed 9 Oct. 1772 from Samuel Elis for £10 sterling and the natural love and affection that he has for his son Solomon, assigns part of tract called *Friendship,* containing 110 acres. Signed b mark before William Luckett, Ans Campbell. Mary Ellis, wife of Samuel Ellis released dower rights.

394-395. James Sprigg of Prince George's County, recorded deed 9 Oct. 1772 from Richard Sprigg for £300 Inspection Currency, parcel willed by Colonel Edward Sprigg, deceased, to be sold, called *Addition to Peters Delight,* signed before Adam Steuart, William Deakins Junr.

395-396. Ninian Willett recorded deed 9 Oct. 1772 from Evan Jones for £100 sells part of a tract of land called *Jone's Lot,* containing 100 acres. Signed before Charles Jones, David Lynn. Ann Jones released dower rights.

396-398. Joseph Conn of Prince George's County, recorded deed 9 Oct. 1772 from John Forest Davis & Lodowick Davis for £335, Two tracts, part of *Davis Content*, beg. at 12th line of *Resurvey on Benjamin's Square*, and part of *Resurvey on Benjamin's Square,* containing in w hole 370 acres. Signed before David Lynn, Charles Jones. Receipt. Catherine and Ellener examined out of hearing of their husbands released dower rights.

398-399. Thomas Cowen of Berkeley County, Virginia, recorded deed 9 Oct. 1772 from William Duff & Agness Duff his wife. Whereas John Chamberlain, Abigail Chamberlain, James Wilson and Agnes Duff, formerly named Agness Thatcher, by instrument of bargain and sale 10 May 1764 did convey unto the said Thomas Cowen, a certain tract of land called *Captain John's Bottom,* containing 100 acres, recorded in Liber I:524, and noted that at that time, Agnes Duff, then Agness Thatcher was under 21 years without proper authority to sell same, now this indenture is made for 5 shillings. Signed by Adnes Duff, William Duff before Thos Price, Jos Wood.

399-400. Peter Shaver recorded deed 23 Nov. 1772 from Adam Beam for £30..10 sells tract called *Williams Loss,* containing 20 acres. Signed in German script before Thomas Price, Evan Shelby. Catherine wife of Adam Beam released dower rights.

400-402. Jacob Good recorded deed 9 Oct. 1772 from Raphael Taney of Saint Mary's County, assigns *Resurvey on Brother's Agreement,* adjacent to tract conveyed by Edward Diggs and Raphael Taney to Thomas Tasker; to second line of 100 acres of land sold by Raphael Taney to George Camorn, then to corner of lot purchased by John Ross to lot conveyed by Raphael Taney to Jacob Richards, containing 368 acres. Signed by both parties before Jno Reden Junr., John Black. Ellen Taney released dower rights.

402-403. William Miller recorded deed 9 Oct. 1772, between William Duff and Agness Duff of Berkeley County, Virginia, Whereas John Chamberlain, Abigail Chamberlain, James Wilson and Agnes Duff, formerly named Agnes Thatcher, by instrument of bargain and sale 4 May 1764 did convey unto William Miller, 50 acres, recorded in Liber I, folio 538; for 5 shillings reconvey tract of land called *Farewell,* Signed by mark, Agnes Duff, and William Duff, before Jacob Miller, and acknowledged before Thos Price.and Joseph Wood

403-404. Peter Huffman recorded bill of sale 12 Oct. 1772 from Henry Unsell for £4 sterling, that property sold him by Henry Wall, one wagon, four horse gears, five cows, other livestock, wheat and 4 acres of Indian corn, on bill of sale. Signed before Thomas Price.

404. Richard Davis recorded bill of sale 13 Oct. 1772 from Samuel Phillips for £8 sell all my crop of Indian corn. Signed by mark before Hugh Evans.

405-406. Martha Harmon recorded deed 9 Oct. 1772 from Richard Lilley, made 28 September 1772 for £36..10 tract called *Fisherman's Lodge,* beginning at a tract taken up by Leonard Morer called *Hole in the Mountain,* containing 30 ½ acres. Signed before Jos Wood, Thomas Price. Mary, wife of Richard Lilly released dower rights.

406-408. John Kennedy recorded deed 19 October 1772 from William Dent, for £400 part of *Resurvey on Locust Thicket,* containing 159 acres, beginning at mouth of a branch called Luke's Mill Branch, Signed before T. Sprigg Wootton, William Deakins, Junr. Mrs. Verlinda Dent, wife of William Dent, released dower rights.

408-409. Thomas Cramphin recorded mortgage 19 Oct. 1772 from George Hoskinson. Indenture made 12 Sept. For £12..8 in dollars at 6 shillings per dollar, assigns tracts in Frederick County where Charles Hoskinson deceased lived, *Elizabeth's Delight, Squabble,* part of *Jenny and Molly,* in all containing 113 ½ acres; provided nevertheless that if George Hoskinson, son of Charles, pays sum, sale is void. Signed before Robert Peter, Adam Steuart.

409. Thomas Sheppard recorded bill of sale 21 Oct. 1772 from Samuel Phillips, for £35, one Negro wench, Nan, provided nevertheless that if I pay or cause to be paid sum by 16 Nov. Ensuing, bill of sale is void. Signed by mark before Anthony Webb, Christopher Culp.

409. Conrad Snider recorded assignment of debt of £38 from George Kyssinger.

410. John Madden recorded release from Wm Murdock Beall 22 October 1772, for bill of sale for Negroes, whereas the said John Madden's father, John Madden has taken it upon himself to pay Wm M. Beall.

410. John Stull and Peter Bainbridge recorded power of attorney 11 Nov. 1772 from Martha Terrence, late Mary White of Cumberland County, Pennsylvania, executrix of John White, appoints attorneys to sell property. Signed by mark.

410. Charles Jones recorded bill of sale 10 Nov. 1772. I James Hutchcraft, farmer, for £8 sell one brindle cow and calf now in possession of Thomas Maynard; also the field of corn now growing on the plantation I rent from Christian Stoner. Signed before Geo Joules.

410-412. John Stull recorded deed 5 Nov. 1772, made 2 Sept. From Lawrence Owen, son of Edward, and Sarah his wife, for £30 tract called *Rubbish,* beginning at a tract called *Discovery,* containing 84 acres. Signed Lawrence Owen, Sarah Owen, before T. Sprigg Wootton, David Lynn.

412-413. John Rhodes recorded assignment of lease 4 Nov. 1772 from Frederick Herring. Whereas by indenture and lease made between Edward Lloyd Esq., of the land office, and George Humboldt, 29 Sept. 1765 for parcel called *Littleworth,* containing 100 acres. Agreement to transfer to John Rhodes.

413-414. Anthony Sell recorded deed 18 November 1772, from Sarah Brice, executrix of John Brice late of Annapolis, for £250, tract called *Exchange,* containing 920 acres. Signed before Jno Brice, Wm Steuart.

414. John Boone of Pennsylvania recorded deed 16 Nov. 1772 from Zachariah White for £1..17, for parcel called *This or None,* beginning at 10 line of *Fellowship,* containing th 9 acres more or less. Signed before Charles Jones, Wm Deakins.

415. William Willcoxon of Prince George's County, recorded deed 16 Nov 1772 from Henry Allison, made 27 October, for £348, *Allison's Adventure* with Resurvey thereof, containing 190 acres. Signed before Adam Steuart, Wm Deakins Jr. Elizabeth, wife to Hendry Allison released dower rights.

416-417. Adam Neff recorded deed 14 Nov. 1772 from Christian Kneiss, for £40, tract called *Deep Hole,* on Shanandore Mountain, containing 45 acres. Signed in German Script before Jos Wood, Aeneas Campbell, Magdalena Kneiss released dower rights.

417. Benjamin Cornall recorded acknowledgment 8 Nov 1772 from Thomas Belt III in Anne Arundel County. The land by the name of *Chance,* was intended to be the same conveyed as *Joseph's Chance.*

418. Conrad Hayberger recorded deed 14 Nov. 1772 from John Miller for £80 sells lot #5 in Sharpsburgh Town. Signed by mark before Jos Wood, Jos Wood Junr. Catherine wife of John Miller released dower rights.

418-420. Daniel of St. Thomas Jenifer of Annapolis, gentleman, recorded deed 21 Nov 1772 from William Reynolds of the City of Annapolis, hatter, for £3..18 sterling, part of *Resurvey on Mitchell's Range,* containing 213 acres. Signed before R. Ghiselin, Wm Stewart.

420-421. Frederick Stemble recorded deed 20 Nov. 1772 from John Harmon Yost for £5 lot in Middletown. Signed German Script before David Lynn, Thos Price. Magdalena Yost, wife of John Harmon Yost released dower rights.

421-422. George Schertzel recorded deed 20 November 1772 from Valentine Stickle of Frederick Town, weaver, for £5 assigns part of lot in Frederick Town, #110 on the south west corner of Market Street, Signed in German Script before Thos Price, John Stull, Thos Schley. Receipt. Sybella Stickles wife of Valentine released dower rights.

422-423. Peter Crowle recorded deed 23 Nov. 1772 from Valentine Flegle in consideration of 15 acres of *Molly's Industry,* assigns the like quantity of 15 acres in *Spring Garden.* Signed by mark before Jos Wood, Thos Price.

423-425. Martin Keplinger recorded release of mortgage 23 Nov. 1772 from John Coonce. Whereas Johnn Coonce by his deed of mortgage made 20 Nov. 1767 for £150 tract called *Parks Hall,* adjacent to Hugh McGragh's part of said tract containing 111 acres, that the same indenture recorded in Liber L:122 to be of no effect. Signed Martin Keplinger, before Jno Stull, Thomas Price.

425-426. Adam Quoranfleece recorded deed 23 Nov. 1772 from Leonard Stephens, for £30 for 107 1/4 acres of land assigns part of tract called *Friendship.* Metes and bounds given. Signed in German Script before Thos Price, John Stull. Elizabeth Stephens, wife of Leonard Stephens released dower rights.

426-428. Samuel Warner Jr. of Prince George County, recorded deed 22 Nov 1772 from Josiah Wilson for £160 Part of tract of land called the *Subrock* (Suburbs) ? 100 acres more or less. Signed before Jos Wood, Charles Jones. Jemima, wife of Josiah Wilson released dower rights.

428-429. Jacob Good recorded land commission and depositions 22 Nov. 1772 on *Skipton & Craven*, appointed William Beard, Christopher Burkett, Van Boarer and Jacob Gaines of Frederick County, requested before Thomas Prather and his associates, that any two of them may take testimony. Signed by T. Sprigg, clerk. Depositions taken from George Markle, regarding spanish oak. John Rife, solemnly affirmed his testimony regarding spanish oak near Jacob Good's saw mill; Frederick Markle, being sworn, saith he was a chain carrier when the surveyor made a survey on part of *Skipton and Craven*, and they ran it from an old spanish oak near Jacob Good's saw mill.

429-430. Arthur Nelson recorded land commission 22 Nov. 1772 on *Hobson's Choice*, Appointed Wm Luckett, Jonathan Wilson, Jno Wilson and Wm Norris for Arthur Nelson's petition 20 August to perpetuate bounds before Thomas Prather. Elias Delashmut aged 61 years or thereabouts swore that about 39 years ago he was present with John Nelson upon an Island in the Potomac River, called at that time *Long Island*, and upon the north side of the Island near the bank, was a tree the aforesaid Nelson told the deponent was the bounded tree of his tract called *Hobson's Choice,* signed by mark. Deposition of Ashman Jenkins aged 39 years or thereabouts, says that about 10 or 11 years ago he was present at the running of the lines of a tract called *Hobson's Choice*, and surveyor Hepburn began at the very tree mentioned in Mr. Delashmutts above as the beginning bounding of the tract.

431-433. John Fletchall recorded land commission 22 Nov. 1772 on *Tom's Last Shift*. Commissioners appoint Nathaniel Magruder (of Alex), Zachariah Magruder, Hezekiah Magruder and Nathaniel Magruder (of Nat), applied for before Thomas Prather. Depoisiton taken of John Collings, aged 59 said that about 24 years ago he was walking in the woods, and found a bounded white oak, which is now the stump we are at, it being 8 yards from a branch known by the name of the Lay Branch, and saith further that after meeting with Jas Tomlinson, told him that the bounded white oak was the beginning or second tree of Richard Lee's land. Saml Magruder 3rd aged 60 years, being sworn, said that at a place known by the name of Tomlinson's Ford on Rock Creek, in the year 1731 or 1732 in company with John Flint Junr., the said Flint pointed up the creek to a white oak about 10 years from the said Ford and told him it was a bound tree of Fletchall's land. James Fife, aged 43 years being sworn, that a white oak stump about 88 years from a branch known as the Lay Branch, that about 19 years ago, Jno Tippet cut down the tree of the said stump for hoops and about 4 or 5 years after the said Fife was — for by Col. Geo Beall and Beall told the depondent that he had cut down the beginning tree of Lee's land, and deponent remembered that John Tippet had said the there was notches on one quarter of the said tree, so that it would not make hoops. Alexander Beall aged 52 years and upwards, after being sworn, saith that when he was a lad his father had a tract of land called *Clain Course*, and that the line run somewhere on the south. Zachariah White aged 35 years, first sworn, at white oak stump standing about 88 yards from a branch known by the name of the Lay Branch, about 3 ½ feet from a white oak standing to the westward of stump, sayeth that 12 or 14 years ago, he being in partnership with Robert Beall to take up land on Rock Creek, who stated that some years ago he was riding up the road with Col. Bradford, and showed Beall the tree of Fletchall's lands, and the white oak was the beginning tree. Some time after he got Hugh Tomlinson to go with him to the beginning of Carroll's land, and as they were walking Tomlinson told him he would show him the beginning tree of Fletchall's land and they went to a place something like the place where the above stump is, and further says that Tomlinson told him that James Fife cut down the tree. Samuel Beall Senr., aged 64 years and upwards, was sworn at said stump, and said the he really believed it was the beginning tree of *Poor Tom's Last Shift,* , but would not swear and further says he gave Jno Flint 10 shillings to show him the tree. Geo Beall Senr. Aged 77 years, sworn, deposeth that some years past he was desired by Richard Lee Esq., to perpetuate the bounds of several tracts of land, and one tract taken up by Thomas Fletchall called *Poor Toms Last Shift*, and deponent went to John Flint to enquire of him about the beginning of tract, and told him that he could not well direct him any more than the end of the last line of *Poor Tom's Last Shift*, was exactly where the main road crosses the Creek for the upper side of the road called Tomlinson's Ford, and could not find the bound tree. Taken 25th Sept. 1772.

433-434. John Snavely recorded deed 16 Nov. 1772 from Robert Rose of Hampshire County, Virginia, formerly of Frederick County, Maryland, for sum of £70 assigns tract called the *Wellwisher,* adjacent to tract called *Tonoloway Lick,* belonging to John Snavely, and formerly to James Dawson on Little Tonoloways, containing 50 acres. Signed by Robert Rose before Evan Shelby, Jno Stull. Johanna Rose, wife of Robert Rose released dower rights.

434-435. Conrad Heyberger recorded 14 Nov. 1772 John Miller for £1 assigns two lots in Sharpsburg Town, lots #12 and #18. Catharine wife of John Miller released dower. Witnesses: Jos Wood, Jos Wood Junr.

435-437. Joseph Ludshaw, miller, recorded deed 16 Nov. 1772 from Peter Olar, shoemaker, for £10 lot being part of *Resurvey on Brother's Agreement,* laid out for 5 acres, near Taney Town, lot #9 in said town. Signed Peter Olar before Wm Blair, Jno McKinley. Elizabeth, wife of Peter Olar released dower rights.

437-438. Joseph Ludshaw recorded deed 16 November 1772 from Peter Olar, for £50 lot on main street on road from Frederick to Taney Town, being lot #6. Signed Peter Olar before Wm Blair, Jno McKinley. Elizabeth, wife of Peter Olar released dower rights.

438-439. Joseph Wells recorded deed 16 Nov 1772 from Thomas Wells of Baltimore County for £5 sterling, *Resurvey on Jacob's Well,* 110 acres. Signed before Andrew Buchanan, William Cooley. Elizabeth Wells released dower rights.

439-440. Michael Stricker, weaver, recorded deed 11 Nov. 1772 from Albright George for £23 *White's Delight,* 25 acres. Signed by mark before Jos Wood, John Wood. Margaret George released dower rights.

440-441. Joshua Beale (or Riale) recorded deed 16 November 1772 from John Stevenson, weaver, for £280 part of *Brother's Agreement,* signed before Martin Adam, George Clark. Acknowledgment and Ann Stevenson released dower rights before Wm Blair, Jos Wood.

441-443. Thomas Talbott recorded deed 20 Aug. 1772 from William Coats for £150 two tracts called *Veatch's Loss,* and *Oversight,* signed before Robert Peters, William Deakins Junr. Mary Coats released dower rights.

443-444. John Boone recorded deed 16 Nov 1772 from James White for £10 sterling, *New Addition,* adjacent to *Good Luck,* and *Fellowship,* signed before Charles Jones, Wm Deakins Junr. Eleanor, wife of James White released dower rights.

444-445. Peter Strine recorded deed 16 Nov. 1772, made 17 Oct. 1772 from William Smith, for £82 tract called *Bushey Neck,* on side of Ellis Branch a draught of Little Pipe Creek, containing 50 acres. Signed before Jos Wood, Jno Middagh. Mary Smith, wife of William released dower.

445-446. Casper Lockman recorded deed 17 Nov. 1772 from Frederick Frazier (or Fraze) for £120 Pennsylvania, tract called *Fenwick (Fennick)* on Kittoctin Creek, 50 acres and tract called *Ridge,* containing 9 acres, and *Bealls Good Will,* beginning at top of hill near Samuel Grable's plantation, that adjoins *Fennick,* for 30 acres. Signed German Script before Thos Price, John Stull. Margaret Fraze released dower rights.

446-447. Joseph Compton recorded lease 17 Nov. 1772 from Henry Clagett for 100 acres on *Quench Orchard,* in consideration of rents in tobacco, per number of workers employed, to be limited to family. Signed before Adam Stewart

447-448. Edward Turner recorded deed 17 Nov 1772 from James White for £49..10 part of *Pleasant Hills,* line on *Fletchall's Good Will.* Signed before Charles Jones, Andrew Heugh. Eleanor White released dower rights.

448-449. James Fraser recorded deed 17 Nov. 1772 from John Campbell Sr. of AAC, for love and affection for his nephew, son of his sister Margaret, tract of land on waters of Linganore, adjacent to Joseph Wood Senior's land, from Philip Boyer's spring at Talbots Branch. Also tract called *John's Delight.* Signed by mark before Basil Burgess, H. Ridgely.

449-450. Adam Ground recorded deed 18 Nov. 1772 from Jacob Good for £75 *James Fancy,* 150 yards from branch of Little Antietam, containing 50 acres. Signed before John Stull, David Lynn. Susanna Good released dower rights.

450-451. Henry Turner (or Ferour) and Jacob Herbaugh recorded mortgage 18 Nov. 1772 from Philip Coon (Kuhn); for £21..14 part of tract called *Pleasant Valley,* on road from Frederick Trace to Rhoderick's. Contains 50 acres. Signed in GS before Thomas Price, James Carroll.

451-452. Robert Peter recorded deed 11 Nov. 1772 from William Batman of Fairfax County, for £40 lot #60 in Georgetown. Signed before Wm Deakins Junr., Adam Stewart.

452-453. Charles Beall recorded 19 Nov. 1772. Made 21 Aug. 1772 between William Littlefield, for 100 pounds currency, sells part of First and Second Resurvey on land called the *William and John*, beginning at end of 95th line of 2nd resurvey, 140 acres more or less. Signed Wm Littlefield. Before Jos. Wood, Thos Price. Aug. 21, 1772, receipt. Deed ack., and at same time Rebecca Littlefield released dower rights.

453-454. Andrew Beall recorded 19 Nov. 1772, made 21st, 1772, between William Littlefield, for £600, sells parcel included within the lines of the Second Resurvey of the tract called the *William and John*, beginning at end of the 13th line of said Resurvey, and running with the lines of the said Second Resurvey to the end of 91 perches on the 91st line, then by a straight line to the beginning containing 687 acres of land more or less. Signed William Littlefield, before Thomas Price, Joseph Wood. Rebecca Littlefield released dower. [Marginal note: April 25, 1783, Exam'd & delivered by commissioner to Ninian Beall.]

454-455. [Marginal note, examined & delivered to his son Andrew.] Recorded by Ninian Beall, son of Ninian, 19 Nov. 1772. made 21st, 1772, between William Littlefield, for £100, part of *Resurvey on William and John*, beginning at end of 52 perches in the 10th line, containing 99 acres more or less. Signed William Littlefield before Thos Price, Jos. Wood. Deed ack., Rebecca Littlefield released dower.

455-456. Margaret Heckman recorded deed 23 Nov. 1772 from John Harris Junr. of Frederick County, for £100 parcel called *John's Delight,* to include 200 acres more or less. Signed before David Lynn, Upton Sheridine. Elizabeth Harris released dower rights.

456-457. Colon Dunlap, & son, recorded bill of sale 17 Nov 1772 from Joseph Stallings made 14 Nov. 1772, for £122..14 sells one Negro woman named Hannah, one Negro girl named Rose, one mulatto girl named Prisse, one Negro boy named Charles, one Negro girl named Nell and Negro boy named Toby; nevertheless provided that if the said Joseph Stallings pays the sum with interest by 1773, sale is void.

457-458. Henry Staley recorded deed 19 November 1772, made same date from Joseph Staley and Jacob Staley, sons of Jacob Staley deceased, and Henry Staley, also son of the aforesaid Jacob Staley. Whereas Jacob Staley by his will and testament bequeath to his three sons the following tracts, *Switzerland* and the *Resurvey on Ohtersham,* deed of partition of real estate. Signed Joseph Staley, Jacob Staley.

458-460. Jacob Staley recorded deed 19 November 1772, made same day from Henry Staley and Joseph Staley, all sons of Jacob Staley, deceased. Whereas Jacob Staley by his will and testament bequeath to his three sons, tracts, and ordained his beloved wife Margaretha, executor, but she refused and took thirds instead, the following tracts are now being divided, *Switzerland* and the *Resurvey on OthersHam,* deed of partition. Signed Joseph Staley, Henry Staley.

460-462. Joseph Staley recorded deed 19 November 1772, made same day between Jacob Staley and Henry Staley, Whereas Jacob Staley by his will and testament bequeath to his three sons, tracts, and ordained his beloved wife Margaretha, executor, but she refused and took thirds instead, the following tracts are now being divided, *Switzerland* and the *Resurvey on Others Ham,* deed of partition. Signed Jacob Staley, Henry Staley.

462-463. Ambrose Cook recorded deed 19 Nov. 1772 from William Dent for £105, parcel containing 53 acres called *Needwood,* beginning at a tract called *Granby,* and running thence to tract called *Rattlesnake,* tence to tract called *Charle's Chance,* and part containing 100 acres. Signed before Wm Deakins Junr., T. Sprigg Wootton. Verlinda Dent released dower rights.

463-464. Joseph, William, Basil and Osborne West recorded deed of partition 22 Nov 1772, made 11 November 1772. Whereas the said Joseph West Junr., William West Junr., Basil West and Osborn West, did by the last will and testament of their father, John West, late of Frederick County, deceased, become seized jointly in a tract of land called *Two Brothers,* containing 200 acres more or less, on the head of a branch called Watts Branch, make partition of the land into 50 acre parcels. Signed by the four parties.

464-465. Christian Shirock recorded release 21 November 1772, that we Matthias Shriock and Barbara his wife, for £34 assigns 47 acres, it being one half of a certain tract of land called *Isles Mountain,* where the aforesaid Chrn Shrioch now lives, together with all appurtenances and advantages thereon, which tract was granted unto Christopher Nofsinger, now deceased, father tot he said Barbara Shriock wife of the aforesaid Mathias Shriock, bearing date 10 November 1752. Mathias Shriock signed in German script, Barbara signed by mark before Jos Stull, Thos Price.

465. Benjamin Cornall recorded acknowledgment 21 November 1772 in Anne Arundel County, before the justice of the Provincial Court, the within named Thomas Belt, the 3rd, acknowledged that the land and premises within conveyed by the name of *Chance*, at the time of conveyane thereof, may have been conveyed by the name of *Joseph's Chance*, and the property is the same Benjamin Carroll's.

465-466. Thomas Owen Williams recorded deed 23 Nov. 1772 from John Hutchinson made 13 November for £28 tract of land called *John and Roses,* beginning at fourth line of tract called *Resurvey on Plain Dealing,* granted unto Aaron Prather, containing 20 acres. Signed by mark before David Lynn, Adam Stewart. Receipt. Acknowledgment. Rose Hutchinson released dower rights. AF paid Wm M. Beall.

466-468. William Renner recorded deed 22 Nov 1772 from Jos Wood Jr. and Robert Wood, made 19 Nov. 1772 for £23 sells 50 1/4 acre part of *Resurvey on Buck Range,* and *Wickhams Discovery.* Signed Robert Wood, Joseph Wood Junr., in presence of Joseph Wood and Charles Jones. Catherine Wood and Ann Wood, wives of Robert and Joseph released dower rights.

468-469. George Zimmerman recorded deed 23 Nov. 1772 from Joseph Hardman, Henry Hardman, sadler, and James Humbert, baker, for 5 shillings, assigns lot #4 [in Frederick Town]. Rents paid to Daniel Dulaney. Signed in German script ___ ____, Henry Hardman, Jacob Humbert (GS) before David Lynn and Thomas Price.

469-470. Wm Robertson and Elizabeth his wife and Ann Robertson, daughter of William and Elizabeth, recorded deed of gift 23 Nov. 1772 from Ann Crabb in consideration of natural love and affection, and 5 shillings, assigns two tracts, part of *Snowden's Manor Enlarged,* and *Evans Rest,* contiguous to each other, and to part of *Charles and Benjamin,* and one line of *Batchelor's Forest,.* Deed to William and Elizabeth for their lifetime, and the longest liver of them, and then to Ann Robertson. Signed before Richard Duckett Jr., John Crow.

470-471. Valentine Flegle recorded deed 23 Nov 1772 from Peter Crawle, deed made 17 Nov. 1772, for 15 acres of tract called *Spring Garden*, assigns the quantity of 15 acres of *Resurvey on Molly's Industry.* Signed Peter Crowl before Jos Wood, Thos Price.

471. Joseph Wood Jr recorded deed 23 Nov 1772 Baltzel Reeme for £10 sells 1 3/4 acre *Bottom Lot,* part of *Spring Plains,* signed by mark, "B.R." before Jos Wood, Charles Jones. Catherine Reeme wife of Balser released dower rights.

472-473. Anthony Boley recorded deed 23 Nov. 1772 from George Fleck for £12 lot #249 in Frederick Town. Signed in German script before Jos Wood, Charles Jones. Elizabeth Fleck released dower rights.

473-474. Thomas Matthews of Virginia, Francis Matthews of Anne Arundel County and David Matthews of Berkeley County, Virginia, sons of Ann; recorded deed 23 November 1772, made 17 Nov 1772 from Wm Schooley of Loudoun County, Virginia and Ann his wife, late Ann Matthews, widow and relict of Daniel Matthews, late of Frederick County, deceased. A tract in Frederick County containing 163 acres, surveyed in 1746, recorded in Ann Arundel Co. Book B1 and BY no. 3, folio 601[47], granted Thomas Matthews, by his deed, 14 Nov 1750, recorded in Frederick County

---

[47] There seems to be a problem with both this patent reference and the deed references. Several patents were granted to Thomas Matthews of Baltimore County, including two in what was then Prince Georges; one *George's Discovery,* contained 175 acres, granted 26 March 1746 recorded in BT/60; the other *Matthew's Lott,* contained 100 acres, granted 29 Nov 1742, recorded in LGB/350; LGE/6t. In Frederick County, Daniel Matthews patented *Daniel's Addition,* for 25 acres 9 Feb 1750 recorded In BY3/346; BY5:596. Liber K, in Frederick County deeds is much later.

book K, folio 317-318[48] to above named Daniel Matthews deceased. Surveyed in 1753 for 163 acres, and by his last will and testament dated 2nd month 1754.[49] Signed William Schooley by mark, Ann Schooley before David Lynn, Thomas Price.

475 Otho Holland recorded deed 23 Nov. 1772 from Archibald Edmonston Jr. For £35. Part of parcel called *Clean Drinking*, beginning at 29th line of *Resurvey on Long Bottom*, to *Batchelor's Hill*, containing 72 acres. Signed before Thos Price, John Chrisman. Ack. AF paid Wm M. Beall.

476-477. Andrew Black recorded deed 23 Nov. 1772 from Heugh Scott for 5 shillings, grants tract called *Butler's Gift*, containing 50 acres. Signed before David Lynn, Adam Stewart.

477-478. George Lutze recorded deed 23 Nov. 1772, made 19 Nov. From Leonard Panther for £82 land containing parts of three tracts conveyed by Wm Sparks to Christian Nisswanger, and Niswanger unto Leonard Panther, part of *Addition to Brookes Discovery on the Rich Lands*, 27 acres; part of *William and Ann*, ½ acre and part of *Spark's Delight*, for 2 ½ acres. Signed in G.S. before Thomas Price, William Luckett. Catherine wife of Leonard Panther released dower rights. AF paid.

478-479. Henry O'Hara recorded deed 23 Nov. 1772 from Peter Hesson for £85 part of *Resurvey on James' Fancy*, beginnning at tract of land called *Long Acre*, for 60 acres. Signed G.S. before Jos Wood, Charles Jones. Christian Hesson released dower rights.

479-480. Adam Stukly recorded deed 23 Nov. 1772 from Valentine Stickle for £43 part of lot #110 in Frederick Town. Signed GS before Thos Price, Jno Stull. Sybella Sheckle released dower rights.

480-482. Joseph West, Junr. recorded deed 23 Nov 1772 from Robert Wood and Joseph Wood for 81 acres of tract called *Wickhams Discovery*. Signed before Jos Wood, Charles Jones. Receipt for £475. Catherine Wood, wife of Robert Wood released dower rights. AF paid.

482. John Everley recorded deed 23 Nov. 1772 from Peter Crowl of Frederick County, for £2, tract. Called *Resurvey on Molly's Industry*, beginning at 5th line of a tract called *Spring Garden*, for 11 ½ acres. Signed by mark before Jos Wood, Thomas Price. AF paid.

---

[48] Should be Liber B:317-318. Patricia Abelard Andersen, *Frederick County MarylandLand Records, Liber B Abstracts, 1748-1752* 2nd Ed., Damascus, Md., GenLaw Resources, 2003, pg.34. Daniel Matthews recorded deed 10 Dec 1750 from Thomas Matthews of Baltimore County in consideration of the love and affection he bears to "my son Daniel Matthews" assigned two parts of tract called *George's Discovery*.

[49] Will named four sons, Thomas, Francis, Daniel and Samuel, and unborn child each £6 as they come of age. All real and personal property to wife Ann, also appointed executor. Proved 24 Dec. 1755 by three witnesses, George Matthews Jr., William Matthews, Mary Matthews. Abstract from Donna Valley Russell, *Frederick County Maryland Wills 1744-1794*, New Market, Md.: Catoctin Press,2002. Originally published in *Western Maryland Genealogy*.

483. Michael Snider recorded deed 23 Nov. 1772 from Andrew Rodrock for £42 tract called *Leaning Rock,* for about 50 acres. Signed in German Script before Thos Price, John Stull. Catherine Rodrick his wife released dower rights.

483-484. Frederick Hersch recorded deed 23 Nov. 1772 from Thomas Bowles for £60 *Resurvey on No Name,* containing 144 acres. Signed before Thomas Price, John Stull.

484-485. Adam Keplinger recorded deed 23 Nov. 1772 from John Coonce (Kuhn), for , tract called *Park's Hall,* adjacent to Hugh MaGraugh's land, containing 107 acres. Signed by mark before Thomas Price, John Stull. Receipt for £272. Acknowledgment. AF paid Wm M Beall.

485-486. Rudy Bruebach, carpenter, recorded deed 23 Nov. 1772 from Joseph Dyer for £52 sells 134 acres of land, the tract called *Dyers Mill*, beginning at first line of St. Mary's Church land, beginning at bounded land called *Lewis's Luck,* Signed, acknowledged before Jos Wood, Charles Jones. AF paid.

486-487. Christian Miller recorded deed 23 Nov. 1772 from Thomas Gartrill of Anne Arundel County; for £50 sells tract called *Tarr Will*, containing 50 acres. Signed before Thos Price, William Deakins Junr.

487-488. Edmond Riggs recorded deed 23 Nov. 1772, made 19 Nov between John Harris, for £100 tract called *John's Delight,* and known by the name of *Green Boyers*, for 2 ½ acres of land. Elizabeth Harris, wife of the aforesiad John Harris released dower rights.

488-489. Thomas Fisher of York Co., Pennsylvania, recorded deed 23 Nov. 1772, made 7 Nov. from Charles Carroll for £24..4. Tract called *Michael's Luck,* containing 46 acres. Signed before Francis Fairbrother, Thos McCargill.

489-490. Zachariah Ellis recorded deed 23 November 1772, made 17 Nov. from John Harris Sr. for £100 part of *John's Delight.* 146 ½ acres. Signed before David Lynn, Upton Sheridine. Elizabeth Harris released dower rights.

490-491. Normand Bruce recorded bill of sale 23 Nov. 1772, from Peter Robey for £20 assigns quantity of tobacco now in my tobacco house, of 500 pounds, and part in the tobacco house of Peter Barnes of 1500 pounds. Signed before Archibald Boyd, Andrew Bruce.

491. Peter Study recorded deed 23 Nov 1772 from Philip Engleberger/Angleberger, son and heir of Philip Angleberger, deceased, for £54..12, tract, *Wynpanfelt,* containing 16 acres. Signed in G.S. before Thomas Pirce, John Stull. Susanna, wife of Angleberger released dower rights.

492. John Wells recorded deed 27 Nov 1772 from Elijah Hall of Linganore on Bush Creek, for £1..2 all my right to a certain school house on Ths Plummer's land, legally purchased by work there, in shingles, nails and cash, paid to make up equal proportion to the rest of the subscribers. Witness: Chris Cons Robotiau, teacher of school house.

492-493. Nicholas Rhodes recorded release 1 Dec 1772 from Jonathan Wilson on tract, *None Left,* signed before Upton Sheridine, Thomas Price.

493-494. Adam Creager recorded deed 2 Dec. 1772 from Valentine Creager, Jacob Foutz, et.al. Whereas Casper Creager by his will dated 5 September 1763 bequeath to his sons and daughters, Christian Creager, Conrad Creager, Adam Creager, Michael Creager, George Creager, Valentine Creager and Catherine Creager, certain lands, and to son Henry Creager, to be equally divided. He died seized in fee of *Casper's Lot,* 30 acres and 20 acres; *Mount Pleasant,* 150 acres; *Sandy Spring,* 250 acres; *Resurvey on Rinehar's First Choice,* 55 acres. Deed from Valentine, Michael, Conrad, George Creager and Jacob Fout, who married Catherine Creager to Adam Creager for £80. Tract. Dower release by Catherine Fout, Christian wife of Valentine, Mary wife of Conrad and Catherine wife of George Creager.

494-495. Conrad Creager, blacksmith, recorded deed 2 Dec. 1772 from Adam Creager, part of *Sandy Spring,* or *Fancy Spring.* Signed in German Script, Adam Creager before Jos Wood, Valentine Creager. Christian, wife of Adam Creager released dower right.

495-496. Joseph Talbot recorded bond assignment 2 Dec 1772 from Thomas Burgee. Know that Samuel Lynn was bound unto Lawrence Robinson Jr. for sum of £200 in November 1765, to make over a certain tract where Samuel Lynn now lives, known as *Snake Root Thickett,* signed Samuel Lynn by mark before Ths Grove, Wm Ridge. Assignment dated 12 January 1771, to Jno Adamson Barkshire, all right to bond, intent and purpose of my sister's portion, signed Lawrence Robinson Junr, witness: Lawrence Robinson Senr. Assignment dated 16 May 1772, for £65 assigns all interest to Thomas Burgee. Signed Jno Adamson Barkshire. Wit. William M. Beall. 22 August 1772, I assign for £68 all interest in bond to Joseph Talbott. Signed Thomas Burgee. Wit: Christian Edelen.

496-497. Thomas Johns et.al. [Thomas Richardson of Frederick County and Jno Biddle and Clement Biddle of Pennsylvania] recorded deed 3 Dec. 1772 from John Cline of Prince George's County, for £10 part of tract called *Dan,* containing 4 acres beginning at third line of Jno Ridgeway's part. Signed in GS before J. Hepburn. Anna Marlena Cline released dower rights.

497-499. Nicholas Ackerman recorded mortgage 4 Dec. 1772 from Daniel Miller on tract called *Ivey Church.* Agreement to pay yearly rents for term of ten years, and Daniel to build a dwelling house 20 ft. square with a good chimney and floor; and a good barn, and to plant an apple orchard of 100 apple trees; he grants unto Nicholas Ackerman one black mare, one bay mare, two weavers looms, one wagon and gears and one plough and all household goods. Signed Daniel Miller before Thos Price, Upton Sheridine. Receipt for £45 received from Nicholas Ackerman, signed by Daniel Miller.

499. John and Thomas Hartley recorded bill of sale 1 Dec. 1772 from Joseph Wilson, son of Lancelot, for debt of £81..16 and additional sum of 5 shillings, sells one Negro wench, Sue 23 years old and her two children, a boy, Cesar, 3 years old and a girl Phillis 14 months old. Signed before Robert Peter.

499-501. George Robertson of Anne Arundel County recorded deed 8 Dec. 1772 from Joseph Elgar, who is seized of a tract called *Batchelor's Forest.* For £1054 he sells 154 acre part. Margaret, wife of Joseph Elgar released dower rights.

501-502. Robert Owen recorded deed 8 Dec. 1772 from Joseph Elgar, mill wright, made 13 Nov. 1771, for £545..8 sells part of tract *Batchelor's Forest,* and *Resurvey on Batchelor's Forest,* on Rock Creek. Containing 303 acres. Margaret Elgar released dower rights.

502-503. George Barnhart recorded deed 8 Dec. 1772 from George Gillespy Junr for £120 tract called *Stedman's Luck,* containing 100 acres. Signed before Thomas Price, Rebecca Price, Jno Stull. Jane Gillespie released dower rights.

503-504. Edward Ward recorded deed 8 Dec 1772 from Nicholas Rhodes, turner for £25 sells tract called *None Left,* containing 28 ½ acres. Signed before Upton Sheridine, Thomas Price. Jane, wife of Nicholas Rhodes released dower rights.

504-505. Carlton Belt recorded deed 8 Dec 1772 from Richard Davis for £112..10 land called *Gear's Adventure* containing 112 ½ acres. Signed before Wm Luckett, Aneas Campbell. Esther wife of Richard Davis released dower right.

506-507. Michael Cyster recorded deed 8 Dec. 1772 from John Stull for £1500 part of *Resurvey on Stull's Forrest,* adjacent to Morningstar's part of said Resurvey, to land of Jno and Daniel Canade, to James White's part, containing 441 acres. Signed before Thomas Price, Wm Deakins Jr.

507-508. Cutleip Miller recorded deed 8 Dec. 1772, made 5 Dec. From Henry Shover of Frederick Town, blacksmith, for £60 sells part of lot #82 in Frederick Town, the same lot Henry Shover purchased of Henry Bruner. Ann Mary Shover released dower rights.

508-510. Andrew Avey (or Evey) recorded deed 7 Dec. 1772 from John Schnebley for £2 part of a tract called *Cold Weather,* and *Huckleberry Hall,* also known as *Resurvey on Warm Weather,* containing 2 3/4 acres. Louisa Schnebley released dower rights.

510-511.Deed recorded by John Coller 8 Dec. 1772 from John Schnebely, blacksmith, for £30 sold and made over to George Coller, parts of tracts *Cold Weather, Huckleberry Hall*, and *Resurvey on Warm Weather,* containing 51 3/4 acres. Signed before Jno Stull, Wm Baird. Louisa, wife of John Schnebely released dower rights.

511-512. Jno Swank recorded deed 8 Dec. 1772 from Henry Keedy for £40 Penn. currency. Tract. Ann wife of Henry Keedy released dower rights.

512-513. Carlton Belt recorded dee 8 Dec 1772 from Notley Gatton for £87..10 assigns tract called *Gore's Adventure,* laid out for 87 ½ acres. Signed before Wm Luckett, Aeneas Campbell. Receipt, ack. Mary Gatton released dower rights.

513-514. Peter Beckinbaugh (Pickenpaw) recorded deed 8 Dec. 1772 from Jacob Henry, indenture made 23 Nov. Whereas a certain George Matthews had granted him a tract called *The Resurvey on Good Luck,* granted for 312 acres, for consideration of £30 paid by Charles Davis, 21 July did convey 100 acres part of the aforesaid 312 acres by George Matthews, who did convey to a certain Jacob Henry on 9 August 1750. The said Jacob Henry for £100 conveys the 100 acres. Signed by mark before Thos Price, Jacob Klein. Receipt. Ack. AF paid Wm Murdoch Beall.

515-516. Andrew Hoover recorded deed 8 Dec. 1772 from John Schnebely, blacksmith, made 24 Nov., for part of *Huckleberry Hall,* for 28 acres beg. at 5th line of *Resurvey on Warm Weather,* Signed before John Stull, Wm Baird. Receipt for £20. Louisa wife of John Schnebely released dower rights.

516-517. Thomas Taylor recorded deed 8 Dec. 1772 from Peter Beckinbaugh (Peckinpaw) for £190 sells part of *Resurvey on Good Luck,* formerly granted to George Mathews for 312 acres in the whole, granted to Charles Davis 100 acres. Deed contains M&B for 43 acres. Signed in GS before Thomas Price, Upton Sheridine. Barbara Peckenpaugh released dower rights. AF paid Wm Murdock Beall.

518-519. Jacob Good Sr. Recorded deed 8 Dec. 1772 from John Schnebley, blacksmith, for £240 part of *Huckleberry Hall,* for 224 acres beg. at 5th line of *Resurvey on Warm Weather,* Signed before John Stull, Wm Baird. Louisa wife of John Schnebely released dower rights.

519-520. Richard VanDike of Philadelphia County, Pennsylvania, recorded deed 3 Dec. 1772 from Richard Brown, Esq. of York County, Penn., executor of Thomas Glen, late of Frederick County, deceased; for £152..15 assigns 100 acres, part of tract *Maiden's Point.* Signed before Jos Wood, Catherine Wood. Susanna wife of Richard Brown released dower rights.

520-521. Henry Shover, blacksmith, recorded deed 8 Dec. 1772 from Henry Brunner. Whereas Henry Bruner by his deed of bargain and sale 13 August 1748, recorded in Liber B:45-47, lots in Frederick Town. Signed GS before Jos Wood, Chs Jones. Magdalena wife of Henry Bruner released dower rights.

522-523. Thomas Beatty recorded deed 8 Dec 172, made 4 Dec. From Jno Hall of Annapolis, attorney at law, two parts of tract called *Middle Plantation,* metes and bounds given for 100 acre part and 750 acre part of said tract. Signed J. Hall before Wm Hyde, G. Duvall. Acknowledged before J.P. of Anne Arundel County. Wm Stewart, Robt Condon.

524 John Hagarty Jr. On 10 Dec. 1772 recorded deed from Charles Beatty and George Fraser Hawkins, for lot #215 in Addition to Georgetown, on tract called *Knave's Dissapointment.* Martha wife of Charles Beatty and Susan Freeman wife of George Fraser Hawkins released dower rights.

524-525. John Hagarty Sr. On 10 Dec. 1772 recorded deed from Charles Beatty and George Fraser Hawkins, lot #9 in Addition to Georgetown, on tract called *Knave's Dissapointment.* . Martha wife of Charles Beatty and Susan Freeman wife of George Fraser Hawkins released dower rights.

525-526. Martin Ullerick recorded bill of sale 14 Dec 1772 from Conrad Fritz for £3 sells cow and calf. Signed in presence of Thomas Pelly, Thos Price.

526-527. Gilbert Kemp, assignee of Christ. Edelin, recorded deed 15 Dec. 1772 from Joseph Ogle, Benjamin Ogle, Wm Ogle, Thos Ogle and James Ogle. All of Frederick County. Whereas Joseph Ogle, deceased, for consideration mentioned therein, did assign 380 acre part of *Resurvey on Fountain Low,* recorded in Liber E:184-185, and Christopher Edelin on 6 Dec 1763 granted Gilbert Kemp the same 380 acres, recorded in Liber I:19-20, this is to correct metes and bounds on deed. Deed acknowleged by five grantees. Martha wife of Joseph Ogle and Mary wife of James Ogle released dower rights.

527-529. Reverdy Ghiselin recorded deed 15 Dec. 1772 from Joseph Ogle Benjamin Ogle, Wm Ogle, Thos Ogle and James Ogle. All of Frederick County. Whereas Joseph Ogle, deceased, for consideration mentioned therein, did assign 380 acre part of *Resurvey on Fountain Low,* recorded in Liber E:173-175; deed to correct metes and bounds.

529. William Dennis recorded deed 24 Dec. 1772 from Charles Coats for £42..10 assigns tract *Daniel's Discovery.* Signed before Wm Luckett, Wm Luckett Jr. Acknowledged before Wm Luckett, Thomas Price. AF paid Wm M Beall.

530. John Barrick recorded deed 24 Dec. 1772 from Adam Ground, made 16 Nov. 1776 for £35 sells lot #17 in Sharpsburgh Town. Signed in GS before Sam'l Beall Jr., John Stull. Christian Ground released dower rights.

530-531. Michael Stokes, saddler, recorded deed of confirmation 24 Dec. 1772 from Henry Brunner. Whereas Bruner by indenture to Benjamin Yates dated 30 August 1772, recorded in Liber L:474-475, conveyed lot #83 in Frederick Town, the property of Charles Beatty, adjacent to lot #82, confirms title to Michael Stokes. Both signed deed in German Script, before Jos Wood, Chs Jones. Magdalena Bruner released dower rights.

531-532. Jacob Woolfe recorded deed 24 Dec. 1772 from George Dagan, made 26 Nov., for £80 sells lot in Sharpsburgh, the eastern part of lot #18, which Dagan leased from Peter Wise. Signed before Valentine Lemuel, Conrad Smoll. Catherine Dagan released dower rights.

532-533. John Barrick recorded deed 24 Dec. 1772 from Adam Ground. Indenture made 16 Dec. For £100, lot #32 in Sharpsburgh, to pay rents to Joseph Chapline. Signed German Script before Sam'l Beall, John Stull. Christian Ground released dower rights.

533. James Hook recorded bill of sale 24 December 1772 from Jacob Kisner for £20 sells one gun, spinning wheel, frying pan, two basins, three plates, skimmer ladle, flesh fork, pewter teapot, two new blankets and bed tick, one madock, three axes, new plow irons, swingle tree (ther chains, tools) one piece of home made cloth for suit of clothes; one Bible testament, psalm book. Nevertheless, sale is void if sum paid with interest by 1 Nov. Next ensuing.

533-534. Jacob Mock of Cumberland County, Pennsylvania, weaver, recorded deed 24 Dec. 1772 from Adam Grove, of Frederick County, taylor for £145, lot #87, house & improvements in Elizabeth Town; to pay Jonathan Hager, rents. Signed in German script before Jno Stull, Wm Baird. Receipt. Ack. AF paid.

534-535. Absolom Beddo and Richard Sheckles of Prince Georges County, recorded deed of trust 2 Jany 1773. Whereas they purchased of Capt. Daniel Stephenson, contiguous tracts of land, called *Bear Garden Enlarged,* and part of *Deer Park,* and part of *First Mistake,* and part of tract called *Second Mistake;* metes and bounds given for separation and partition of tracts. Signed by both parties before Jos Wood, C.H. Lowndes.

536-537. Absolom Beddo and Richard Sheckles recorded deed of trust 2 Jany 1773, made 5 Sept. 1772, for four tracts, as above, laid out for 397 acres. Made partition. Signed as above.

537-538. Barton Philpott of PGC recorded deed 4 Jan. 1773, made 13 ?Oct. From Adam Stewart of FC, Thomas Montgomery of Prince William Co., Va. And Cumberland Wilson, part of land called *Resurvey on Merryland.* Signed before Robert Peter, William Deakins, Junr. Receipt for £574..15. Ack. AF paid.

538-539. George Scott recorded lease 5 Jan. 1773 from Jane Ridgely widow of Nicholas Greenberry Ridgely, late of AA Co. Deceased of one part, George Scott, one of heirs of George Scott of PGC deceaed, grants tract called *Norway,* on upper side of Seneca Creek, containing 630 acres. Signed Jane Ridgely before Adam Stewart, Wm Deakins, Jr.

539-540. George Scott recorded deed 5 Jan. 1773 Jane Ridgely, widow of Nicholas Greenberry Ridgely, late of A.A. Co.. Deceased, and executor of his will. Signed indenture for same property, per contract previously made by Nicholas Greenberry Ridgely. Metes and bounds given, AF paid Wm M. Beall.

540. John Troxall recorded bill of sale 6 Jan 1773 from John McMahon for £100 sells to John Troxall, Negro man named William about 23 years of age. Signed John McMahon before Wm Blair.

540-541. Michael Buff recorded bill of sale 6 Jan. 1773 from Christian Light for £25 sells one sorrel/roan mare.

541-542. Christian Cruiss recorded lease 8 Jan. 1773 from Joseph Chapline, assigns lot, part of tract called *Joe's Lott,* containing 100 acres. Signed by both parties before Saml Beall Junr.

542-543. Jacob Kisener recorded lease 16 Jan. 1773 from John Trammell, tract of land on branch commonly called Dry Brnach, near where he now lives, for 10 years, to pay 1000 lbs tob. Annually.

543-544. Thomas Polhaus recorded deed 18 Jan. 1773 from Peter Buckey, made 17 Jan., lot which formerly belonged to Joseph Hartman, deceased, parts of Lots #210, 203 in Frederick Town. Signed before Basil Beall, Wm Luckett. Mary Bucky released dower.

544-545. Leonard Beavens recorded deed 17 Jan. 1773 from Jacob Mills, made 29 Dec. 1772, for £211 PA, tract *Beaver Dam Bottom,* granted 20 Oct. 1747. Signed by mark, before John Stull, Wm Baird. Ann Mills, wife of Jacob released dower.

545. Conrad Grosh recorded lease 23 Jan. 1773 from Daniel Dulaney for one penny, assigns lot in Frederick Town, 160 ft. by 390 ft. for one year.

546. Conrad Grosh recorded release 23 Jan. 1773 from Daniel Dulaney, for lot #101 in Frederick Town. Whereas Dan'l Dulaney agreed with Adam Schultz in his lifetime, for lot and AdamSchultz for consideration, assigned lot to Abraham Bear, now deceased, now for convenants herein confirms lot unto said Conrad Grosh.

546-547. Michael Buff recorded deed 23 Jan. 1773 from Christian Light for £200, assigns parcel, *Resurvey on William's Neglect,* M&B for 135 acres. Signed before Wm Baird, Jno Stull.

547-548. Conrad Sheratz recorded bond 25 Jan. 1773 from Michael Buff for £126 bond to make a good deed on tract *Resruvey on William's Neglect.* Signed before Elias Barton, Edmon Jagman (?).

548. William Ray recorded deed 27 Jan. 1773 from Zachariah White. Indenture made 1 Aug. 1772, for £5, assigns tract adj. William Ray's land called *Wet Beginning,* containing 65 acres. Signed before Andrew Hugh, Chs Jones. Mary, wife of Zachariah White released dower rights.

549-550. Patrick McSherry of Germany Township, York County, Pennsylvania, recorded deed 28 Jan. 1773 from Henry Yesler, of the Borough of Lancaster, Lancaster County, Pennsylvania, made 19 Nov. 1772. Whereas Henry Hall of Anne Arundel County, by indenture 21 October 1755, and assigned tract to said Henry Yesler by name of Henry Esler. Signed in German script before Wm Deakins Junr., Thos Price.

550-551. John Bamberger recorded deed 28 Jan 1773 from John Ingram, indenture made 14th December 1772, for £25 Penn., tract called *Virgin Lair,* about 1/4 mile from the tract called *St. Patrick's Lot*, on the south side of the Wagon Branch which leads into Beaver Creek Branch of Great Antietam Creek, M&B containing 58 acres. Signed before Jno Stull, Wm Baird. Elizabeth, wife of John Ingram released dower.

551-552. Henry O'Hara recorded deed 28 Jan. 1773 from Charles Carroll of Annapolis, made 19 Dec. 1772, for £45..19, tract *Long Acre,* on south side of branch called Poplar Run, a draught of Great Pipe Creek. Signed before Francis Fairbrother, Francis Pugh.

552-553. John Miller recorded deed 28 Jan. 1773 from Charles Carroll of Annapolis, made 19 Dec. 1772, for £35..11, tract *Bear Meadow,* containing 155 acres. Signed before Francis Fairbrother, Francis Pugh.

553-554. Bartholomew Keefer recorded deed 28 Jan. 1773 from Charles Carroll of Annaplis, made 19 Dec. 1772, for £73..4, tract, *Tatnum Green,* standing on Bear Branch of Great Pipe Creek, for 100 acres. Signed before Francis Fairbrother, Francis Pugh.

554-555. James Slater recorded deed 28 Jan. 1773, made 20 Dec. 1882 from Jas Maginnis for £70 tract called *Hickman's White Oak,* M&B given in a hollow near Potomac River, for 85 acres. Signed by mark of James Slater, before Aeneas Campbell, Adam Steuart. Charity Slater released dower rights. Alienation fine paid, William Murdock Beall. [there seems to be some confusion here regarding grantor/grantee and who is paying for tract. This may be a type of mortgage deed].

555-556. John Robinson, sadler, recorded deed 28 Jan. 1773, made 16 Jan. From Jacob Hose, joiner for £48, ½ of lot #81 in Elizabeth Town, adjoins NW side of Doctor Henry Schnebeley. Signed before Wm Baird, Jno Stull. Margaret wife of Jacob Hose released dower.

556-557. Benjamin Notley Price recorded deed from Charles Beatty and George Fraser Hawkins, for $6. Lot #289 in Addition to Georgetown, on *Knave's Disappointment.* Signed before Joseph Wood, Thomas Price. Martha wife of Charles Beatty and Susan Freeman wife of George Fraser Hawkins released dower rights.

557-558. George Warring recorded deed 28 Jan. 1773 from William Deakins Jr. For £150 sells tract called *Friendship*, containing 200 acres, beginning at a bounded white oak standing in the west side of a branch called Cattail Marsh. Signed Wm Deakins Jr. Before Adam Steuart, Aeneas Campbell.

558-559. Peter Erb recorded deed 28 Jan. 1773 from William Beall, made 19th Dec. 1772, for £50 tract called *Bell's Choice,* M&B for 54 acres of land. Signed by mark before Jos Wood, Catherine Wood, by her mark. Receipt. Elizabeth wife of William Beall released dower right. AF paid Wm M. Beall

559-560. Samuel Jones of Prince George's County, recorded deed 28 Jan 1773 from Isaac Simmons of Anne Arundel County, for £100 tract called *New Laid Tomahock,* including a tract called *Belt's Tomahock,* originally granted Capt. Jeremiah Belt, for 150 acres and the vacancy added by Isaac Simmons, M&B given for 350 acres. Signed before Thos Watkins and Richard Harwood Junr., deed ack. and at same time Abigail Simmons, wife of Isaac, released dower right. AF paid Wm M. Beall.

561-562. Joseph Brown recorded deed 28 Jan. 1773, made 14 Dec.1772 from Henry Keedy, for £400 assigns sells part of tract *Mon Him,* beginning at bounded hickory on south side of the Wagon Branch, a draught of Antietam and near *Rattle Snake Denn*, between Matthew Clark and the south ridge of a mountain, M&B given for 150 acres. Signed in German Script before Jno Stull, Wm Baird. Ann, wife of said Henry Keedy released dower rights. AF paid Wm M. Beall.

562-563. Thos Taylor recorded deed 28 Jan. 1773, made 13 Dec. Between Thomas Matthews, Daniel Matthews of Loudon County, Virginia, Francis Matthews of AAC, for £69 tracts adjoining each other, called part of *George's Discovery*, and part of *Resurvey on George's Discovery,* to 4th line of *Daniel's Addition,* containing 11 acres. Signed by all three parties before Thos Price and Sam'l Irwin. Receipt, acknowledgment, AF paid.

563-564. Conrad Show, taylor, recorded deed 28 Jan. 1773, made 30th December 1772 between Thos Matthews of Loudon County, Virginia, Francis Matthews of Baltimore County and Daniel Mathews of Loudon County, part of tract called *Resurvey on George's Discovery,* granted Daniel Matthews 4 August 1752, and part of *Daniel's Addition,* containing 73 acres; also a second part of tract called *Daniel's Addition,* for 14 acres. Signed by all three before Thos Price, Sam'l Irwin.

565. Thomas Gaver recorded deed 28 Jan 1773 from Joseph Plummer, made 4 Dec. 1772 for £25 assigns 100 acres of part of tract, *Land of Promise,* Signed before Sam'l Beall Junr., John Stull. Receipt. Ack. AF paid.

566. Thomas Johns recorded deed 1 Feb. 1773 from Thomas Cleland of Calvert County, for £100 assigns tract of land in Georgetown, lot #24 togethr with dwelling house and outhouses. Signed before David Lynn, Wm Deakins Junr.

566-567. Joseph Sim recorded deed 6 Feb. 1773 from Addison Murdoch and John Murdoch, of PGC, for £2000 assigns tract *Addison's Choice,* it being 1/3 part of said tract of land, which was supposed to contain764 1/4 acres together with all houses, out houses, buildings, gardens, orchards and meadows, common pastures, woods, waterways, easements, profits, commodities, advantages, entitlements, and hereditments whatsoever. Signed before Robert Peters, Adam Steuart. Receipt. Acknowledgment. AF of 30 shillings, 7 pence, and 1 farthing by order of Daniel of St. Thomas Jenifer, Esq. received by Wm M. Beall.

567-568. John Belt recorded deed 6 Feb. 1773 from Daniel Carroll of Frederick County, for £187 assigns tract called *Grandmother's Good Will,* standing at head of draft of a branch called Ten Mile Creek, laid out for 150 acres. Signed before Robert Peters, Adam Steuart. Receipt. Ack.

568-569. Christian Foglesong recorded deed 6 Feb 1773 from Jacob Funck, indenture made 3 Feb. For 7 shillings, assigns lot #11 in Jerusalemtown. Signed before Robert Peter, Adam Stuart. Ann wife of Jacob Funck released dower rights. AF paid.

570-571. Jacob Sharrer recorded deed 6 Feb. 1773 from Jacob Funck, indenture made 3 Feb. For 7 shillings, 6 pence, assigns lot #123, in Frederick County on plat of town. [Jerusalemtown ? Not named]. Signed before Robert Peter, Adam Stuart. Ann wife of Jacob Funck released dower rights. AF paid.

571-572. Conrad Sheratz of York County, Penn., and Sam'l Irwin, recorded mortgage 9 February 1773, indenture made 8th February, from Michael Buff for £83 conveys parcel called *Resurvey on William's Neglect,* M&B given for 137 acres, provided always that if the said Michael Buff pays with full sum in common circulating currency, by 30th August next, with legal interest, this deed is void. Signed in GS before Thomas Price, John Stull. Ack.

572-573. John Campbell Jr. Recorded deed 8 Feb. 1773 from John Campbell Sr. of Anne Arundel County, made 9 Oct. 1772, for love and affection he had unto his God Son John Campbell Junr., and 5 shillings, tract called *John's Good Luck,* containing 130 acres more or less. Signed by mark before Basil Burgess, Charles Gassaway. Ack. AF paid.

574-575. Abraham Miller recorded deed 14 Feb. 1773, indenture made 11 February 1773 between Jacob Miller. Whereas the said Abraham Miller and Jacob Miller had on 17 August 1766 a tract called *Miller's Choice,* containing 432 acres, being part of the *Resurvey on Welch Cabin,* to them as heirs and assignees of their father, Adam Miller, recorded in land records Liber H:688-690, for

£5 for 216 acres. Signed before Jos Wood, John Wood. Hannah Miller wife of Jacob Miller released dower rights. Acknowledgment.

575-576. Jacob Miller recorded deed 14 Feb. 1773, indenture made 11 February 1773 between Abraham Miller. Whereas the said Abraham Miller and Jacob Miller had on 17 August 1766 a tract called *Miller's Choice,* containing 432 acres, being part of the *Resurvey on Welch Cabin,* to them as heirs and assignees of their father, Adam Miller, recorded in land records Liber H:688-690, for £5 for 216 acres. Signed in German Script before Jos Wood, John Wood. Mary Miller wife of Abraham Miller released dower rights. Acknowledgment before Jos Wood, Thomas Price.

576. Joseph West Jr. recorded lease 15 Feb. 1773 from Nathaniel Offutt of Samuel for £40 assigns tract called *Younger Brother,* on Watts Branch, containing 100 acres, assigns from this date for 21 years. Signed by both parties before David Lynn, T. Sprigg Wootton.
576(a) -577. [misnumbered 576] Joseph Hitechew recorded lease 16 Feb 1773 from Saml & Bennett Chew of Anne Arundel Co., in consideration of rents, covenants & agreements herein, assigns 100 acres of land, part of a tract called *Chew's Farm,* lot #11. Signed Sam'l Chew, Bennett Chew, Joseph Hitechew before R. Ghiselin, Robert Condon.

577-578. Joseph Hitechew recorded lease 16 Feb 1773 from Saml & Bennett Chew of Anne Arundel County, assign for term of 21 years, parcel #20 on *Chews Farm.* To build a house, 20 feet by 15 feet, with feather edge shingles, and also within six years plant an apple orchard of 100 fruit trees. Signed Sam'l Chew, Bennett Chew, Joseph Hitechew before R. Ghiselin, Robert Condon.

578-579. Casper Smith recorded bill of sale, 20 Feb. 1773 from James Young for £31 sells two cows, and benefits which I have of a lease from Daniel Dulaney for 50 acres of land called *the Forrest,* and all the grain now growing. But should I by 1st November next ensuing pay the sum above with interest, sale is void. Signed by James Young in presence of Elias Barton and Sam'l Irwin.

579-580. Thomas Gaunt Jr. of Prince George's County, Recorded deed of exchange 22 Feb. 1773 from Thomas Gaunt Sr. on *Hawkin's Merry Peep a Day,* which tract Thomas Gaunt bought of George Frazer Hawkins, containing 1550 acres, assigns tract in exchange for tract lying in Prince George's County, called *Seat Pleasant.* Signed Thomas Gantt, before Jno Hepburn, John Smith Brookes.

580-581. Thomas Taylor recorded deed 22 Feb. 1773, made 1 Feb. Between Leonard Smith of Frederick County, for £26..11..6 part of a tract of land that Fielder Gantt took up, called *Bayley Spring,* and now called by the name of *Mistaken Rival,* M&B for 16 acres, clear of elder surveys. Signed before Wm Luckett, Jonathan Wilson. Elizabeth Smith, wife to Leonard released dower rights. AF paid Wm Murdoch Beall.

581 John Creale recorded deed 24 Feb. 1773, made 8 Feb 1773 from Elias Barton of Frederick Town, for 5 shillings assigns a certain half of lot #2, in Frederick Town. Signed by both parties before Thos Price, John Stull. Anne Barton wife of Elias Barton released dower rights. AF paid.

581-582. Michael Stricker recorded deed 24 Feb. 1773, made 21 Oct. 1772, from John Cochran, weaver, for £10 for tract, *Addition to John's Child,* for 18 acres, and a second part of 7 acres beginning at *John's Child,* signed before Wm Blair, Wm Blair, Jr. Ack. AF paid.

582-583. Jacob Rohrer recorded deed 24 Feb. 1773 from William Deakins Jr. For £40 sells part of *Frenches Contrivance,* M&B on line of *George's Mistake, Georges Venture and the Barrens,* containing 30 acres. Signed before Robert Peter, Adam Steuart. Ack. AF paid.

583-584. Martin Adams recorded deed 24 Feb 1773 from Samuel Andrews for £400, part of *Addition to Brookes Discovery on the Rich Lands,* to the bank of Piney Creek, for 200 acres. Signed before Wm Blair, Jno Patterson. Sarah wife of Samuel Andrews released dower.

584-585. John Yates recorded deed 21 Feb. 1773 from Andrew Leitch, Francis and William Deakins Junr., for £85, 89 1/4 acres of *Conclusion,* and 24 acres of tract *Fat Bacon,* signed before Jos Beall, Chr Lowndes. Margaretha Augusta Leitch, wife of Andrew released dower.

585-586. Abraham Faw recorded deed 24 Feb. 1773 from Orlando Griffith for £125, sells one acre of tract called *Adams Bones,* signed before Wm Luckett, Thos Price. Elizabeth wife of Orlando Griffith released dower rights.

586-587. George Martten recorded deed 24 Feb. 1883. Made 15 Jan. From Wm Deakins, Jr. For £50 assigns part of *Resurvey on Chaney's Delight,* containing 40 3/4 acres. Signed before Robert Peter, Adam Steuart.

587-588. Thomas Lancaster Lansdale made deed 10 Oct. 1772 from Isaac Lansdale of PGC. Whereas Thomas Lansdale did in his life time settle on them a tract called *Easy Purchase,* Signed before Joseph Sprigg, Richard Duckett Jr. Eleanor wife of Isaac Lansdale released dower.

588-589. Benj. Dulaney, Esq., Daniel Dulaney and James Marshall, recorded performance bond for £1000, 2 May 1773 from the Right Hon the Lord Proprietory, to secure him while he continues in office of clerk and record keeper of Frederick County.

589-590. Robert Strawbridge recorded deed 8 March 1773 from John England Sr., made 2 March for £50 sells part of *Brother's Inheritance,* and part of *England's Choice,* M&B given for 50 acres, adjacent to *Pork Hall.* Signed before Upton Sheridine, Thos England.

590. John Glassford & Co. Recorded deed 8 March 1773 from Abraham Benjamin for £10 assigns tenement called *The Discovery,* for 85 acres leased to Abraham Benjamin 9 Jan. 1769 for 21 years. Signed by mark before Robert Peters, Rob't Ferguson.

590-591. John Glassford & Co. Recorded bill of sale 8 March 1773 from Abraham Benjamin. I Abraham Benjamin for £38..15 money due John Glassford & Co., assign 3 cows, 7 sheep, 15 hogs, one mare about 7 years; one horse, two feather beds, 9 pewter plates, 4 pewter dishes, 2 pewter basins, 3 iron pots, one Dutch oven, signed by mark before Robt Peter, Robt Ferguson.

591-593. John Glassford & Co., merchants, recorded deed 8 March 1773 from Nathaniel Magruder son of Ninian. Whereas Nathaniel Magruder owes and is indebted in the sums of 18,463 pounds of heavy crop tobacco at Rock Creek Warehouse, and £382..18 for dealing at the store in Georgetown, he assigns tract willed to him by his father, called *Resurvey on part of Honesty,* 101 acres, of part of *Friendship,* since resurveyed and called *Magruder's Purchase,* and also five Negro slaves, one man called Cook, one called Aaron, one boy called Cook, one woman called Page and one wench called Hannah. Provided nevertheless if that the sums are paid with interest by first January next, sale is void. Signed before Robert Peter, Wm Deakins, Jr.

593. James Ellis recorded deed 8 March 1773 from Samuel Ellis, for £5 sterling, sells part of tract called *Friendship,* containing 149 acres. Signed by mark before Wm Luckett, Aeneas Campbell. Mary Ellis wife of Samuel Ellis released dower rights.

593-594. John Myers recorded deed 8 March 1773 from John England for £170 sells part of tract called *Brother's Inheritance,* containing 83 acres. Signed before Upton Sheridine, John England Jr.

594-595. Samuel England recorded deed 12 March 1773 from John England Sr., made 1 March for £50 sells part of *Brother's Inheritance,* on line with *England's Choice,* containing 111 acres. Signed before Upton Sheridine, John England Jr.

595-596. John England Jr. Recorded deed 12 March 1773 from John Miers (Myers), made 2 March for £70 sells a parcel of land called *Ridgeway's Farm,* M&B for 13 acres. Signed in German Script, before Upton Sheridine, Sam'l England.

596-597. John England Jr. Recorded deed 12 March 1773 from John England Sr., for £50 part of *England's Chance,* and *Ridgeway's Farm,* containing 102 acres. Signed before Upton Sheridine, Sam'l England.

597-598. Henry Hill recorded deed 12 March 1773 from William McCarthy, made 15 Jan. 1773 for £25 tract called *Mountain Glade,* on Catocktin Mountain, containing 30 acres of land. Signed before Thomas Price, Thos Beatty. Elizabeth wife of William McCarthy released dower rights.

598. Martin Line recorded sale 12 March 1773 from George Fogle for £4 sells one white cow about 6 years old. Signed in German script.

598-599. John Middlekauf recorded deed 15 March 1773 from Philip Gesler, made 3 March 1773 for £22 Penn. Assigns ½ of lot #36 in town of Sharpsburg. Signed in GS before Jno Stull, Sam'l Beall Junr.

599-600. Peter John recorded deed 15 March 1773, made 8 March 1773 from John Henry Ridenour for £80 assigns parcel called *Ridenour's Lot,* on first line of a tract called *Jacob's Well,* laid out for 40 acres. Signed G.S. before Jno Stull, Wm Baird. Catherine wife of John Henry Ridenour released dower rights.

600-601. Peter Crowle recorded mortgage, 16 March 1773 from Henry Alspaugh for £30 for two lots #22 & #23, in the town of Westminster, Signed in German Script before Thos Price.

601-602. Robert Ferguson and Adam Stuart recorded deed 17 March 1773 from Jeptha Hollingsworth, stone mason, for £200 assigns lot #30, in Georgetown. Aseneth, wife of Jeptha Hollingsworth released dower rights before Robert Peter, Wm Deakins Junr. AF paid.

602-603. Ludwick Butts/Putts recorded deed 17 March 1773 from John Wootring. Whereas Lawrence Creager patented tract called *Resurvey on Longatepaugh,* and sold tract to Jno Daniel Wootring (as Warthing) in deed recorded in liber K, folio 194-195; and he sold parts to John Wootring in deed recorded in liber N folio 72. M&B given for 14 acres. Signed before Joseph Wood, Charles Jones. Elizabeth Wootring, wife of John released dower rights.

603-604. Benjamin Hall recorded deed 17 March 1773 from Mary Hall. Whereas Benjamin Hall late of Frederick County, deceased, by his will bequeath to his wife Mary Hall, tract called *Resurvey on Hall's Choice,* for £150 sells tract containing 100 acres. Signed before Thos Price, Philip Albright.

604-605. Jacob Carn (Karn) recorded lease 17 March 1773 from John Chisholm, school master, for 2 shillings lets tract, part of *Josburgh (?) Forest*. Containing 50 acres, at a corner of John Calleman's land, to let for 20 years, paying annual rents of £2..10 and to plant an orchard of 50 apple trees within 10 years. Signed Jacob Karn, John Chisholm before Upton Sheridine, Wm Luckett.

605-606. John Callaman recorded lease 17 March 1773 from John Chisholm. from John Chisholm, school master, for 2 shillings lets tract, part of *Josburgh (?) Forest*. Containing 50 acres, to let for 20 years, paying annual rents of £2..10 and to plant an orchard of 50 apple trees within 10 years. Signed before Upton Sheridine, Wm Luckett.

607. Peter Tysher recorded mortgage 18 March 1775, made same date from Doctor Thomas Polhouse for £84 parts of lots #199, 200, 201, 202, 203, 204, 205 & 206, in Frederick Town, to adjoin lots which formerly belonged to Joseph Hardman, deceased. Provided always that is sum paid with interest, this indenture is void. Signed before Wm Luckett, Wm Deakins, Jr.

608. Isaac Cooper recorded deed of confirmation 17 March 1773 from John Stull. Whereas by indenture of bargain and sale, recorded in Liber N, folio 13, part of *Resurvey on Stull's Forest*, adjacent to *Resurvey on Old Fox Deceived*, and the *Saw Pitt*, deed confirmed for 107 acres. Signed before Wm Been, Evan Shelby. Receipt for £500.

609-610. William Pack recorded lease 18 March 1773 from Henry Clagett, on tract called *Quince Orchard*, for 100 acres, to hold from 25 Nov. 1772 for 16 years to pay 7000 lbs. Of tobacco in casque at Georgetown Warehouse, each year, plus additional amounts if adult workers other than the family's minor sons and daughters and his wife, worked on the crop. He was also to build what is commonly called "a bastard framed tobacco house"[50] to be built within 5 years, 32 feet by 32 feet, covered with shingles; and to plant an orchard of 100 apple trees. Signed before Robert Peter, Adam Steuart.

610-611. James Langton recorded lease 18 March 1773 from Edward Villars Harbin of Prince George's County. Two tracts on Rock Creek, a part of *Addition to Fellowship*, and *Johnny's Poplar Spring*, for 21 years, with dwelling house. Signed before Robert Peters, Adam Steuart.

611-612. George Waters recorded deed 18 March 1773 from Jacob Wise for £85 tract called *Grandfather's Gift*, beginning at the 9th line of said tract, M&B given for 50 acres. Signed by mark before Michael Cresap, Jno Stull. Wife (name blank) of Jacob Wise released dower rights.

612-613. Adam Steuart of Frederick County and others [Thomas Montgomerie and Cumberland Wilson of Prince William County, Virginia, merchants] recorded deed 18 March 1773 from Hector Ross of Fairfax County, Virginia, made 20 Oct. 1772, for £4,600 Sterling of Great Britain, tract of land called *Merryland*, standing on Potomac River, a little below Shanandoad Mountain, for 6300 acres. Hector Ross signed before Robert Peter, Wm Deakins Junr.

613-614. Hector Ross of Fairfax Co., Va., merchant, recorded deed 18 March 1773, made 12 Oct. 1772 between Adam Stewart of Frederick County, Va., Thomas Montgomery and Cumberland

---

[50] Garry Wheeler Stone, "Society, Housing, and Architecture in Early Maryland: John Lewger's St. John's" (January 1, 1982). Dissertations available from ProQuest. Paper AAI8307366. "Their product was the "bastard" or "lap work" building, a structure whose sills were raised off the ground on cedar or locust blocks, but whose walls and roofs were framed without expensive mortise and tenon joints."

Wilson of Prince William County, Virginia, merchants, for £4,600 tract called *Merryland,* beginning at bounded ash on bank of Potomac, for 6300 acres. Signed by three parties before Robert Peter, Wm Deakins Junr.

614-615. Normand Bruce recorded bill of sale 18 March 1773 from Jacob Ogle for £42..5 sells one red cow, 4 yrs old; two 2 year old heifers and other livestock. Nevertheless if sum paid with interest, bill of sale is void. Signed before Geo Dickson, Robert Pottens.

615. Lancelot Jacque and Thomas Johnson Junr. of Annapolis, recorded deed, as tenants in common, 18 March 1773 from Robert Harrison for £42..14 tract called *Roses Neglect,* containing 39 acres and *Long Island,* containing 21 acres more or less, and *Good and Bad,* containing 15 acres. Signed before Jno Stull, Ths Sprigg Wootten. Receipt. Acknowledgment.

616. John Glassford & Co., Alexander Cunningham and others recorded bill of sale 19 March 1773 from Francis Gilbert for £241..18..5 sells Negroes Charles, boy Tom, boy Ben or Benjamin, boy Harry, Wench Paul (Poll) and Mary, girl Nan; one bay horse, other livestock and furniture enumerated, provided nevertheless, that if sums paid, sale is void. Signed before Wm Luckett, Alexander Magruder.

616-617. Thomas Welsh recorded bill of sale 7 March 1773 from Cornelius Conn for £17..4 for 12 acres of grain in the ground on said Welch's plantation. Signed before Peter Grosh. Acknowledged before Wm Deakins.

617. Jonathan Hager and William Baird recorded bill of sale from James Knox, waggoner, for £30 sells one wagon and four hourses, to pay sum before 20 July for redemption of bargained goods. Signed before John Stull.

617-618. Robert Harrison recorded deed 18 March 1773 from Ezekiel Cox for 16 shillings, tract called *Good and Bad,* on the main road from Fort Frederick to Petersborough, containing 15 acres. Signed before Evan Shelby, John Stull. Sarah Cox released dower rights.

618-619. Samuel Ennis recorded lease 19 March 1773 from Thomas Johnson Jr of Annapolis. Assigns for 21 years, in consideration of rents and covenants, herein, *Resurvey on Hickory Thickett,* M&B for 100 acres, to pay rental sums, and convenants including plant an orchard of 100 apple trees. Signed before B. Johnson, Robert Peter.

619-620. Thomas Spalding recorded lease 19 March 1773 from Thomas Johnson Jr. of Annapolis, for rents and covenants herein, assigns part of *Three Springs,* M&B for 100 acres. Signed as before.

620-621. Ignatius Simms recorded lease 19 March 1773 from Joseph Helms for rents and covenants, herein, assigns tract, *Resurvey on Charles Mount,* containing 69 acres. Signed before Thos Price, Robert Peter.

621-622. Henry G. Dorsey recorded lease 17 March 1773 from Samuel Chew and Bennett Chew of Anne Arundel County, for rents and convenants herein, assigns 100 acres of *Chew's Farm,* signed before R. Ghiselin.

622-624. Francis Deakins on 19 March 1773 recorded deed from Charles Beatty and George Fraser Hawkins for lots #259 and others on Market Street, in Addition to Georgetown, on *Knave's Disappointment.* Martha wife of Charles Beatty and Susan Freeman wife of George Fraser Hawkins released dower rights.

624. Jno Stoner recorded bond 20 March from Jacob Stoner, bound for £300 made over to Philip Hammond of Anne Arundel County, parcel called *James Delight,* in AAC containing 90 acres, the said Jacob Stoner will bear all costs, and damages from John Stoner. Signed before Jos Wood, Peter Smith.

624-625. Henry Crowley recorded release 20 March 1773 from Gabriel Isenbergh (Eisenbergh). Bound in a special warranty with Jno Sweednigler, released and quit claimed before Robert Peter and David Lynn.

625. Henry Crowle recorded release 20 March 1773 from Gabriel Isenbergh (Eisenbergh). In a bargain and sale 23 March 1769, Gabriel Eisenback was bound; it is intention to release his heirs against a certain Edward Digges, or any of them. Signed Henry Crowle before Robert Peter, David Lynn.

625. John Heyster and Edward Fitzgerald recorded bill of sale 21 Mch 1773 from William Bloyce for £160 and 3000 lbs crop tob., sells four feather beds and furniture, 4 pewter basins, 6 pewter plates, one dish, one linen wheel, 9 head of cattle, 9 head of sheep, 4 lambs, 32 hogs, 3 chairs, 2 tables, one chest, one trunk, 2 horses, 2 guns, 4000 lbs. Tobacco, one looking glass, 2 wedges, 2 grubbing hoes, 5 broad hoes. Signed by mark before Chas Jones, Clem Beall.

625-627. John Grimes recorded lease 20 March 1773 from John Chisholm for tract, *Schargh ? Forest,* M&B given for 50 acres. Signed before Thos Reynolds, Mary Stewart.

627-629. John Glasford & Co. recorded mortgage 21 March 1773 from Erasmus Gill Jr. for £385..2..5, and also other sums, four tracts called *Barnaby,* granted Erasmus Gill for 305 acres; tract called *Cloun Close,* conveyed by Charles Carroll to him for 23 3/4 acres; tract conveyed by Joseph Bell of Prince Georges Co. For 12 ½ acres; and part of *Chevy Chase,* conveyed by Ths Bell 3rd for 49 acres more or less. Also certain Negroes, man Limbo and Tom, lad Will, boys Nace, Harry, Bob, Jacob and Jere and girl named Jannes. Signed Erasmus Gill before David Lynn, Robert Peter.

629. Samuel and Daniel Hughes recorded deed 20 March 1773 deed from Wm Deakins for £5 tract called *Good Friday,* adjacent to *Resurvey on Chester,* signed before Robert Peter, Adam Stewart.

630. Francis Deakins and Wm Deakins recorded deed 20 March 1773 from Samuel Hughes, iron master, for £100 tracts on Conococheague Creek, *The Rubicam,* 52 acres; *Pleasant Mount,* 68 acres, *Standby,* 84 3/4 acres, and other tracts, 13 in all, containing 814 1/4 acres. Signed before Samuel Beall, Thomas Price.

630-632. Daniel Sybert recorded deed 22 March 1773 from Christian Leatherman for £150 tract called *Shady Grove,* beginning at *Gaver's Garden,* M&B for 200 acres. Signed in GS before Samuel Beall, Wm Deakins Jr. Barbara Leatherman released dower rights.

632. Joseph Nicholson of Cumberland County, PA, recorded deed 22 March 1773 from Christopher Shockey for £150 PA, *Resurvey on Sarah's Delight,* 100 acres. Signed in GS before Jno Stull, Wm Beard.

632-633. Adam Coil (Koil) recorded deed 22 March 1773 from John Ieam for £50 parcel called *Worse and Worse,* on east side of south mountain, south of main road from Frederick Town to Fort Frederick. Signed GS before Jno West, Chs Jones. Christina, wife of Jno Iam released dower. AF paid Wm M. Beall.

633-634. Henry Shriock recorded deed 22 March 1773 from Jonathan Hager, for lot #97 in Elizabeth Town. Signed before John Stull, Wm Baird.

634. Henry Wigell recorded deed 22 March 1773 from Jonathan Hagar for lot #97 in Elizabeth Town. Signed before Jno Stull, Wm Baird.

634-635. Matthias Saylor recorded deed 22 March 1773 from John Brown for lot #82 in Elizabeth Town, to pay rents to Jonathan Hager. Signed before John Stull, Wm Baird.

635-636. John Sybert recorded deed 22 March 1773 from Jacob Rise for £200 for tract called *Red Liquor,* on east side of Beaver Creek. Signed by mark before William Davison, John Stull. Ann Rise released dower rights.

636. Jacob Bier and Charles Weaver recorded deed 22 March 1773 from Thomas Dorsey of Anne Arundel County for £140. Lot #18 in Frederick Town. Signed before Sam'l Beall Junr., Robt Peter. Receipt, Acknowledgment. AF paid.

636-637. Richard Hoggins recorded deed 22 March 1773 from William Deakins Jr. for £5 tract *Conclusion,* beginning at tract called *Discovery,* containing 100 acres. Signed Wm Deakins Jr. Before Robt Peter, Adam Stewart.

637-638. James Fleming recorded deed 22 March 1773 from Philip Miller for £300, tract called *Isaacs Range,* also *Resurvey on Isaac's Range.* Signed before Sam'l Beall Jr., Thos Price. Receipt. Acknowledgment. AF paid.

638-639. Christian Hamblin recorded deed 22 March 1773 from Jacob Winroad for £100, tract called *Frederick Hill,* containing 74 acres. Signed by mark before Jos Wood, Wm Blair. Receipt. Acknowledgment. Barbara Winroad released dower rights.

639-640. Philip Oster recorded deed 22 March 1773 from Jonathan Hager for lot #126 in Elizabeth town. Signed by both parties before John Stull, Wm Baird.

640. Francis Ratcliffe recorded lease 22 March 1773 from Samuel Hanson of Charles County, for 21 years, parts of *Resurvey on Three Groves, Yorkshire,* and part of *James and Mary,* containing 307 acres, the first parcel of John Moore, and the other two of John Dickerson.

640-641. George Coller Sr. Recorded deed 22 March 1773 from John Hoover of Frederick County for £20, *Resurvey on Nicholas Mistake,* originally granted Henry Hall deceased, 29th Aug. 1761, since conveyed by his son, Henry Hall Jr. To John Hoover. M&B for 11 ½ acres. Receipt, Acknowledgment, Mary Hooker released dower. AF paid Wm Murdock Beall.

642. Jacob Lance recorded deed 22 March 1773 from David Owens for £30 for *Woodstock Forest,* M&B for 50 acres. Signed before Jos Wood, Thos Price. Acknowledgment.

642-643. Michael Reiss (or Acres) recorded deed 22 March 1773 from Leonard Shown, tract called *Mill House,* 23 acres. Signed in GS before Wm Baird, John Stull. Mary Shown released dower rights. AF paid Wm Murdock Beall.

643-644. Michael Aons (or Rerer) recorded deed 22 March 1773 from Lenard Shown for £100 se;;s tract. *Resurvey on Hibernia,* containing 13 ½ acres. Mary wife of Leonard released dower rights.

644-645. Adam Coil (Koil) recorded deed 22 March 1773 from John Ieam for £50 sells tract called *The Gap,* for 50 acres. Signed in G.S. Cristina, wife of John Iam released dower rights.

645. Jacob Adams recorded deed 22 March 1773 from Thomas Gilbert for £20 assigns lots in Frederick Town, #199, 200, 201, 202, 203, 204, 205, 206 unto said Jacob Hoover (or Adam?). Signed before Jno West, Wm Blair. Elizabeth Gilbert released dower rights. AF paid.

646. James Beall, son of James recorded deed 22 March 1773 from Zachariah Beall for £100 200 acres of *Wet Beginning.* Signed before Charles Jones, Wm Deakins Jr. Rebecca, wife to Zachariah Beall released dower rights.

646-647. Ann Collins recorded deed 22 March 1773 from Sarah Shaw, seized in 200 acres of tract called *Peace and Plenty,* by the last will and testament of her former husband, Joseph Ogle, deceased, for £3 sells one acre, M&B given. Signed by her mark before Sam'l Beall Jr., Thos Price.

647-648. Peter Wertz recorded deed 22 March 1773 from George Zimmerman for £200, assigns *Resurvey on Lashmonts Folly,* adjacent to *Joseph's Hills.* 154 3/4 acres. Signed before Jos Wood, Chs Jones. Receipt, ack. AF paid.

648-649. Christopher Brown recorded deed 22 March 1773 from Philip Miller for £20, tract called *Legacy,* containing 50 acres. Signed before Sam'l Beall Jr. Catharine, wife of Philip Miller released dower.

649-650. Philip Stamback recorded deed 22 March 1773 from Christopher Shockey, for £5 Penn. Assigns tract, *Resurvey on Sarah's Delight.* Signed in GS, receipt, acknowledgment, AF paid.

650. James Shriock recorded deed 22 March 1773 from Jonathan Hager for lots 136, 137, 138 in Elizabeth town. Signed John Stull, Wm Baird.

651-652. Henry Smith recorded deed 22 March from George Shisler for £400 tract *Pick All,* patented to Bartholomew Bougher, the whole tract called *Long Dispatch,* beginning at *John's Delight.* Signed GS before Jos Wood, Charles Jones. Receipt. Ack. Margaret, wife of George Shidler, released dower. AF paid.

652. Michael Eckerd recorded deed 22 March 1772 from Leonard Showne for £200 tract called *Carroll's Range,* containing 120 acres. Signed before John Stull, Wm Baird. Mary Shown released dower rights.

652-653. Isaac Cannady (or Knadrick) recorded deed 22 March 1773 from Jonathan Hagar, lot #102 in Elizabeth town. Signed before John Stull, Wm Baird.

654-655. John Hoover recorded deed 22 March 1773 from William and Sarah Watson, executor and executrix of David Watson, deceased. Whereas indenture of bargain and sale 13 May 1769, for consideration therein, and £100 paid by Michael Miller, parcel called *Harvey's Grove,* containing 140 acres, obtained deed of conveyance from David Watson. Sarah signed by mark, Wm Watson signed before John Stull, Wm Baird. AF paid.

655-656. Francis Deakins recorded deed 22 March 1773 from Thomas Johns for £5 assigns lot called *Wellment,* beginning at 10 line of *Resurvey on Chester,* containing 310 th acres. Signed before Wm Deakins Jr. Sarah Johns released dower. AF paid.

657-658. Christian Eder recorded deed 22 March 1773 from Christian Leatherman for £50, part of *Shady Grove,* M&B for 132 acres. Signed GS before Sam'l Beall Junr., Wm Deakins Jr. Receipt, ack. Barbara Leatherman released dower. AF paid.

658-659. Peter Heffler recorded deed of confirmation 22 March 1773 from Isaac Kendrick (or Knadrick), for lot #102 in Elizabeth town. Signed by mark before John Stull, Wm Beard.

659-662. John Hoover recorded deed 22 March 1773 from George Coller Sr. for £20 sells tract, *Hall's Sale,* granted George Coller, 27 Sept. 1769, beginning at 6th line of *Resurvey on Michael's Mistake,* granted to Henry Hall. Signed in GS before Wm Baird, John Stull. Barbara Coller released dower rights.

662-663. Christopher Brown recorded deed 20 March 1773 from Philip Miller for £50 part of *Isaacs Range,* containing 40 acres. Signed before Sam'l Beall Junr., Thomas Price. Catherine Miller released dower.

663-665. Joseph Jones recorded deed 22 March 1773 from Henry Cole for £240 sells two tracts, *the Two Brothers,* on Licks Branch, 200 acres, originally granted Thomas and John Fletchall, and also *Coals Purchase,* adjacent to *Two Brothers,* containing 120 acres. Signed before Wm Luckett, Aeneas Campbell. Mary Ann Cole released dower.

665-666. Samuel Waters recorded deed 17 March 1773 from John Waters of Prince George's County, for £2..12, *Water's Purchase,* adjacent to *Water's Gift,* M&B given to Patuxent River, containing 52 acres. Signed by mark before Dan'l St. Thos Jenifer, John Carroll.

666-667. Samuel Waters recorded deed 17 March 1773 from John Waters Jr., for 5 shillings and love and affection for my son Samuel, assigns part of *Bear Neck,* and *Marion's Fancy.* Signed by mark, appears same as above.

667-668. Christian Crall recorded deed 20 March 1773 from Christian Stover for £140 sells part of *Resurvey on Shoemaker's Knife,* 54 acres. Signed before Jos Wood, Thos Price. Mary Stover released dower rights.

668-669. Mathias Need recorded deed 22 March 1772 from Jonathan Hager for lot #133 in Elizabeth Town. Signed before John Stull, Wm Baird.

670. Henry Miller recorded deed 22 March 1772 from Jonathan Hager for lot #72 in Elizabeth Town. Signed before John Stull, Wm Baird.

671-672. George Smith recorded deed 22 March 1772 from Jonathan Hager for lot #32 in Elizabeth Town. Signed before John Stull, Wm Baird.

672-673. Christopher Brown recorded deed 20 March 1773 from Laurence Delaughter for £40 sells parcel *Agreed in Time,* containing 50 acres. Signed before Sam'l Beall, Thos Price. Barbara DeLaughter, released dower rights.

674-676. John Heinkee recorded deed 24 March 1773 from John Wootring. Whereas Lawrence Creager patented *Resruvey on Longatepaugh,* and also *Schemamner,* and *Stony Corner,* all of which he conveyed to Dan'l Wootring, in deeds recorded in Libers K:194-196, 196-198 and in Liber N folio 72; now John Wootring for £300 assigns 121 acres adjacent ot Lodowick Pottes part of the *Resurvey,* adjacent to High Run, to 7th course of Enoch Frye's part, and also 48 acres of *Stony Corner.* Signed before Jos Wood, Charles Jones. Elizabeth Wootring released dower rights.

676-677. Chester Whiteman of Lancaster county, Pennsylvania, recorded deed 22 March 1773 from Henry Reidenaur for £50, tract called *Whiteman's Prospect,* for 776 acres. Signed German Script before Wm Baird, John Stull. Wife (not named) released dower.

677-679. William Robertson recorded 22 March 1773, land commission and depositions, issued to John Baker, Zadok Magruder, Wm Waters, and Thos Owen Williams. Whereas Robertson is seized of a tract called *Owen's Rest,* he petitioned the court 23 Dec. 172 to perpetuate the memory of the bounds. Deposition of James Brooke, aged about 68 years, solemnly affirmed that about 9 years ago, Edward Owen deceased, who was a chain carrier at the surveying of *Owen's Rest,* told deponent that the tree they wer enow at was the beginning tree. By virtue of the above, the commission, on 23 Jan. 1773, marked the small black oak stump about 10 feet high, with one notch and blaze on east side of it, on ridge in the fork of the Northwest Branch, near line of tract called *Charles and Benjamin.*

679-680. Catherine Toms recorded commission and deposition. Whereas she is seized of a tract called *Toms Folly,* she petitioned Justice Thomas Prather of the court to perpetuate the memory of the bounds. Deposition of Samuel Toms, told of an old Spanish oak, now blowed down, he knew to be the boundary, now marked with a stone.

680-682. Jacob Bluebaugh recorded commission and depositions relating to *Weedings Choice.* John Logsdon Sr., aged 57 years, said two trees lying on ground always known as boundary. Ralph Logsdon, aged 36 years, said about 20 years ago, he saw two surveyors at the said trees, and they told him they were the bound trees. James White, age 42 years, said that three days after the land was surveyed he was by the two bound trees. Signed before Wm Winchester, John Christman.

682-684. Thomas Graves recorded land commission 22 March 1773 to Kinsey Gettings, Charles Jones, Andrew Heugh and David Lynn, on tract called *Chevy Chase,* petitioned 1 June 1764, commisison issued 25 June 1664. Three advertisements were placed, one at the church at Georgetown, and one at the house of Thomas Graves, being a public house. In Frederick County, 17 July 1772. The following depositions were taken on Friday, 14 August 1772. Henry Allison, aged 65 years deposed that his father John Allison, Jr., told him in company with Capt. Archibald Edmonston and the old Wm Offutt, in going up the county that bound tree standing near the split rock or stone, where we now are, and is the bound tree of old Colonel Dent's land. Signed Hendery Allison. John Moore, aged 60 years or thereabouts, deposed that 22 or 23 years ago he was riding up county with Joseph Belt and James Edmonston, who showed deponent bounded tree standing a little distance westward of the split rock, to be the bounds of *Friendship,* and the corner of *Chevy Chase.* Samuel Beall Sr., aged 65 years, deposed that 30 and 40 years ago, John Rodgers being in company with deponent showed him the split stone or rock, saying it was a stone of consequence, as it was a corner of Addison's land.

684-686. Simon Householder recorded deed 22 March 1773 from George Smith. Assigns lot #32 in Elizabeth Town. Signed before Wm Baird, John Stull. Mary, wife of George Smith released dower.

686-687. Thos Contee and Jno Hanson recorded lease 14 April 1773 from William Luckett for yearly rent of one penny, lot near the stone house where the said Contee and Hanson now keep store, near the dwelling house of William Luckett, and where they are about to build a warehouse. Signed before Francis Deakins, Samuel Lyeth.

687-688. Elias Delashmutt recorded Bill of sale 18 April 1773 from Edward Hose for £40 one rug, one blanket one feather bed. If sum paid, sale is void. Signed before Thos Duckett, Thos Price.

688-689. William Elder Junr recorded bill of sale 22 March 1773 from James Andrews for £15, five cows. If sum paid, sale is void. Signed before Benjamin Ogle Jr., Richard Elder.

689-691. David Mitchell and Joseph Gaither recorded deed of confirmation from Jonathan Hager for deed of bargain and sale recorded in Liber O:33 & 34, for lot #111 in Elizabeth Town, with consideration and covenants therein. Signed before John Stull, Michael Cresap.

691-692. Arthur Nelson recorded mortgage 19 March 1773 from Rinaldo Walker for £44, part of *Resurvey on Virgin's Delight,* to pay sum before 25 December 1773. Signed before Thos Price, Upton Sheridine. Elizabeth Walker, widow and relict of Nathaniel Walker released dower rights.

692-693. Levy Cohan and Samuel Beall, and company, and Mitchell and Gaither, recorded deed 29 March 1773 from Peter Consela for £100 assigns one black horse, one sorrel horse, one red brindle cow one black cow, likewise the lease of plantation where I now dwell. Signed before William Duckett Jr., David Mitchell.

693-694. Philip Fishburn and Jacob Good, innholder, recorded bill of sale 29 March 1773 from Conrad Boner of Taneytown, for £200 due to Mathias Bush in Philadelphia, lot #4 in Taneytown. Signed before John Logsdon, George Clark.

694-696. Townly Bruce recorded deed 14 April 1773, made 2 Nov. 1772, from Notley Masters for £400, tract, *Resurvey on Thorough Fare.* Metes & bounds given for 197 acres. Signed before Conrad Grosh, Thos Price. Margaret Masters released dower rights.

696-698. John Hanson Jr. Recorded deed 4 April 1773 from Adam Linder Coone (Koon) of Lancaster County, Pennsylvania for £315. Lot #28 in Frederick Town. Signed before Paul Zanzinger, Nicolas Hauer.

698-699. John Hanson Jr. Recorded deed 4 April 1773 from Adam Linder Coone of Lancaster County, Pennsylvania, for £100. Lot #21 in Frederick Town. Signed before same witnesses. Jacob Young of Frederick County, empowered to acknowledge deeds.

End of Liber P

Frederick County Land Records Libers S, T and U

The following Abstracts for Liber S, are intended to serve as a more detailed index for genealogy researchers than is available in the traditional courthouse or on-line indexes, as an aid to quickly find records for your ancestors. Names of people, and some land tracts and places are extracted for indexing. If you are interested in any of the following people it is encouraged that you obtain a copy of the deed. At this time, they are available from the county courthouse, and/or from the Maryland State Archives website, and can be printed off from a personal computer. To do so, go on the web site for land records, obtain a password, go to Frederick County section of land records site, and enter Liber letter and folio numbers. Happy hunting.

LIBER S

S:1-3 Abraham Barnes and Richard Barnes recorded power of attorney 30 May 1773 from Barnes and Ridgate to Zephaniah Turner and Joseph Gwin. I John Barnes of Charles County, merchant and partner in trade with Thomas Howe Ridgate of London, merchant, appoint attorneys above to pursue trade.

S:3-23 John Rogers, Francis Stone and Philip Richard Fendall, others recorded deed of trust 30 May 1773 from John Barnes of Charles County, Zephaniah Turner & Joseph Gwinn. By Richard Barnes, et.al., attorneys in fact, for 6 shillings sterling assigns tracts in Charles County: *The Wolf Pit,* 234 acres, and two other tracts; one other tract bought from a certain Peter Wood, called *Woods Low Ground;* tract called *Simpson's Chance,* on west side of *Piles Swamp*, at bound tree of a tract called *Saint Thomas,* a tract called *Calvert's Crose,* originally a boundary of *Saint George,* tract purchased by John Barnes and Thomas Howe Ridgate of a certain John Slye containing 34 acres, and land purchased of Philip Wood in occupation of Philip Briscoe on behalf of the heirs of Francis Parnham, deceased. Lot in occupation of Robert Horner. Also lot 76 acres occupied by Edward Edelen. Lot purchased by Robert Haver with water mill from a certain Jestinian Burch containing 9 acres; also lot in Charestown commonly called Port Tobacco from Samuel Hanson Jr. Lots in Benedict Town. Lot in Georgetown in Frederick County purchased by John Barnes and Thomas Howe Ridgate of Thomas Addison and three lots in Addition to Georgetown from Charles Beatty and George Frazer Hawkins; and five lots or parcels in *Carrollsburgh* in Prince George's County. Also slaves Lucy and her child Jesse, slave Lendau and her two children Sam and Nelly; and slaves Ralph, Bristol, Harvey, Sarah and her children Peg and Cato. And one ship called *Nancy* now on a voyage from Europe to America. Livestock and other items also enumerated.

S:23-26 Simon Miller recorded deed 14 April 1773, from Christian Miller for 5 shillings, part of *Christian's Chance.* Signed by mark before Joseph Wood, Andrew Bruce.

S:26-28 Jacob Michael recorded deed 17 April 1773 from Ann Dickson, lot #127 in Frederick Town, adjacent to John Marquart's part of lot. Signed before Jos Wood, Thos Price.

S:29-31. John Marquardt recorded deed 17 April 1773 from Ann Dickson, part of lot #127 in Frederick Town.

S:31-33. John Allison recorded deed 17 April 1773 from Lawrence O'Neale for £12, tract *Pleasant Mountain,* near head of marsh that leads into Captain John's Branch.

S:34-36. Adam Cresap recorded deed 17 April 1773 from Ann Dickson for £1..13, lots #177 & 178 in Frederick Town, to build house on each lot.

S:36-40. Thomas Elder recorded deed 17 April 1773, made 6 March 1773 from Henry Toms now of "Chamberland County" Pennsylvania. Refers to deed O:597-598, portion of *Stony Meadow,* 20 acres, together with *Gaming Castle* and *All Meadow,* this deed conveys additional vacancy to *Stony Meadow,* granted in BC&GS#42, folio 303, for 98 ½ acres. Signed by mark before John Stull, Wm Baird. Mary, wife of Henry Toms released dower.

S:41-43. David Delauter recorded deed 17 April 1773 from Philip Miller for £10, 30 acres of *Resurvey on Isaac's Range.* Catherine Miller released dower.

S:43-45. Henry Delawter recorded deed 17 April 1773 from Philip Miller for £10, 90 acres of *Resurvey on Isaac's Range.* Catherine Miller released dower, witnesses: Thos Price, Sam'l Beall Jr.

S:45-48. James Duley Jr. Recorded deed 17 April 1773 from James Duley Sr. for £34 *Dooley's Chance,* 34 acres. Signed by mark before Charles Jones, Andrew Heugh. Elizabeth Dooley released dower rights.

S:48-50. Philip Clinger recorded deed 17 April 1773 from Samuel Krybell (Grable) for £10, lot in Jerusalemtown. Hannah Krybell released dower. Wit: Wm Baird, John Stull.

S:50-52. Gilleon Strider recorded deed 12 April 1773 from Joseph Hyndman for £35, lot #38 in Frederick Town. Margaret Hyndman released dower.

S:53-56. John Swann of Hagerstown, recorded deed 17 April 1773 from Joseph Gaither & David Mitchell, merchants for £45, assigns part of lot in Elizabeth Town, adjacent to house of said Gaither. Signed before Michael Cresap, Wm Baird.

S:56-59. Adam Knouff recorded deed 17 April 1773 from John Tucker for £235, *Honesty is Best when Lookt To,* 206 acres. Elizabeth Tucker released dower before Jos Wood, Wm Blair.

S:59-62. Michael Holler recorded deed 17 April 1773, from Doctor James Brand of Frederick Town for £7..5, lot #179 in Additional lots in Frederick Town, which he came to possess by condemnation for him against John Baily in 1769. Ann Brand released dower.

S:62-66. Hugh Scott recorded deed 17 April 1773, made 9 April from Simon Miller for £400, tract called *Hard Grubbing,* 220 acres. Signed mark before Jos Wood, Andrew Brice. Phranna Miller released dower.

S:66-69. Michael Haverly recorded deed 17 April 1773 from Conrad Jacobi for £50 *Grove's Bill,* conveyed by Thomas Johnson to him for 9 acres; also tract *Spittlefield,* adjacent to *Resurvey on Rams Horn,* for 14 acres. AF paid Wm Murdoch Beall.

S:69-70. Michael Haverly recorded deed 17 April 1773 from Sophia Jacoby, who gives bond of £50 that she will confirm to sale made by her husband Conrad Jacobi and gives up right of dower.

S:70-73. Conrad Moser recorded deed 17 April 1773 from Christian Leatherman for £20 sells part of *Shady Grove,* adjacent to Christian Eader's part for 40 acres. Barbara Leatherman released dower.

S:73-77. Jacob Kershner recorded deed from John Volgamott (Wolgamot) for £82. *Amendment,* and *Resurvey on Batchelor's Hope,* 31 ½ acres. Mary Volgamott released dower.

S:77-80. Christopher Wertenberger recorded deed 17 April 1773 from Nicholas Elvesta (Helvesta) for £9, lot #12 in Middletown. Wife [name blank] of Nicholas released dower.

S:80-83. Charles Chaney recorded deed 17 April 1773 from Utella Etchicher for £4 lot #25 in New London.

S83-86. Balthasar Simon recorded deed 17 April 1773 from John Shade for £112, tract, *The Good Wife,* on Tuscarorah Creek, 3/4 mile above Jacob Bank's plantation, containing 87 acres. Signed GS. Catharine Shade released dower.

S:86-88. James Knott recorded deed 17 April 1773 from Joseph Smith of PGC for £400 tract *Hard Struggle.* Signed before Robert Peter, Adam Stewart. Rachel Smith released dower.

S:89-91. James White recorded deed 18 April 1773 from Dr. David Ross of PGC, for £223..6..8, *Addition to Fellowship,* conveyed by Hugh Tomlinson to above parties in partnership with Zachariah White, together with mills, houses, etc. Signed before Jos Beall, Christopher Lowndes. Ariana Ross released dower.

S:92-93. William Reynolds recorded deed 8 April 1773 from George Donnally for £4..13, plantation on Tom's Creek, joing lands of William Shields, belonging to Norman Bruce and others.

S:93-95. Zadock Dickerson recorded deed 21 April 1773 from Surratt Dickerson for £71 part of *Dickason's Lot,* beginning at *John & James Choice* containing 40 acres.

S:96-99. George Michael Eller recorded deed 24 April 1773 from Edward Gaither of Benjamin for £90, part of *Hammond Strife,* near Pipe Creek, 100 acres. Elenor Gaither released dower.

S:99-102. Adam Wolfe recorded deed 24 April 1773 from Edward Gaither, son of Benjamin for £68 part of *Hammond Strife,* on Pipe Creek, 76 acres. Eleoner Gaither released dower.

S:103-105. Francis Deakins recorded deed 21 April 1773 from Martin Hoffman for £1 sterling, lot #81 in Addition to Georgetown, on *Knave's Disappointment.* Signed GS. Barbara Hoffman released dower.

S:105-108. Paul Crouse recorded deed 26 April 1773 from John Rister of Baltimore for £200, *Taylor's Delight,* and *Free Gift,* near Great Pipe Creek. Signed G.S. before Jos Wood, William Bentley. Margaret Rister released dower before Upton Sheridine, Jos Wood.

S:108-112. Paul Crouse recorded deed 26 April 1773 from John Rister of Baltimore, for £30, tract called *Dry Work,* on south side of a ridge, containing 27 acres. Signed as above.

S:112. Malachiah Bonham recorded bill of sale 26 Apr. 1773 from Edward Inman for £13 a black gelding. Signed before Francis Gilbert, John Waters. Ack. before Thomas Price.

S:113-120. Jonathan Hager recorded deed 26 April 1773 from John Rohrer of Lancaster County, Pa., son and heir at law of Jacob Rohrer, for £230 sells parts of three tracts, *Resurvey on Hager's Fancy,* 107 acres; part of the *Second Resurvey on part of Hager's Fancy,* 90 acres, and part of *Dry Pond,* 25 1/4 acres. Signed in G.S. Franey Rhorer, wife of John and Anna Rhorer, widow of Jacob Rhorer released dower rights.

S:120-123. Horatio Sharpe Esq., John Ridout, Esq., Daniel Dulaney, Esq. And Frances Hutchinson, Esq., recorded power of attorney from Frederick Haldeman, of the City of New York, province of New York, to sell several tracts of real estate of which he is possessed in Maryland.

S:123-125. William Patterson, mason, recorded deed 26 April 1773 from Wilfred Neale and Eleanor Digges executors of Edward Digges, late of St. Mary's County, deceased, for £70 part of *Brothers Agreement,* contining 16 acres.

S:125-129. Mathias Ridenour recorded deed 26 April 1773 from Henry Ridenour for £50, *Resurvey on Henry's Last Shift,* Eve Ridenour, wife of Henry, released dower rights.

S:129-136. Jonathan Hager recorded deed 26 April 1773 from John Rohrer of Lancaster Co., Penn., son and heir of Jacob Rohrer, late of Frederick County. For £600, sells parts of six tracts, *Resurvey on Stoney Batter, Addition to Stoney Batter, Second Resurvey on part of Hagers Fancy, Amendment to the Resurvey on Hagers Delight,* and part of *Rhorer's Fancy.* Metes and bounds given, including division line between John Rohrer and his brother Jacob Rohrer. Signed in G.S. before Evan Shelby, John Stull. Franey Rhorer, wife of John and Anna Rhorer, widow of Jacob Rhorer released dower rights.

S:137-143. John Rohrer of Lancaster County, recorded deed 26 April 1773 from Jonathan Hager for £200 part of *Resurvey on Stoney Batter,* containing 30 acres, *The Amendment to Resurvey on Hager's Delight,* and third tract, a part of *Exchange,* 12 acres.

S:143-151. Jacob Rohrer recorded deed 26 April 1773 from John Rohrer of Lancaster County, his brother, for £650, several tracts from Jonathan Hager, and others. Signed GS before Wm Baird, John Stull. Franey Roher, his wife, and Anna Rhorer, widow of John Rohrer Jr., deceased, released dower rights.

S:152-156. Andre Evey recorded deed 26 April 1773 from Jacob French for £150, part of *Huckleberry Hall,* 54 ½ acres. Magdalena French released dower rights.

S:157-160. George Garrett (Gerrick) recorded deed 26 April 1773 from Thomas Weller Sr. For £900, *Little Meadow,* on draught of Potomac, near wagon road from Stull's Mill. Mary Weller released dower rights.

S:160-163. Charles Beatty recorded deed 26 April 1773 from Peter Beard for £5, for lot #79, *Addition to Georgetown,* signed before Jno Wood, Thos Price. Catherine Beard released dower.

S:163-168. Thomas Johns and Thomas Richardson of Frederick County, and James & Clement Biddle of Philadelphia, merchants, recorded deed 26 April 1773 from Daniel Carroll for £17, part of *Joseph Park,* on Rock Creek. M&B for 2 ½ acres. Signed before Adam Stewart, William Deakins.

S:168 Thomas Johns recorded receipt 26 April 1773 from John Ridgeway 26 April 1773. Received of Thomas Johns, by the heirs of John Gregg, the sum of £16..4 in full consideration accorded me by Msrs Clement Biddle and Peter Becraft, for a road through my plantation to

Ths Johns and Ths Richardson's mill on Rock Creek. Signed John Ridgway by mark before Joshua Gregg, Aquilla Johns.

S:168-171. Jacob Marken recorded deed 26 April 1773 from George Turnball for £130, *Resurvey on Owings Chance.*

S:171-174. Jacob Marken recorded deed 26 April 1773 from George Turnball for £240, tract called Ment.

S:174-178. Jno Chris Fauber recorded deed 16 April 1773 from Jacob Fletcher of Taneytown for £80, lot #23 in Taneytown. [or Jacob Good, name within deed]. Signed G.S., Mary wife of Jacob Fletcher released dower.

S:178-182. George Turnbull recorded deed 26 April 1773 from Sam'l Owings Jr. Of Baltimore County, for £39..4, *Resurvey on Owings Chance,* 9 acres, and 2nd parcel, 2 ½ acres. Deborah Owings released dower rights.

S:182-186. John Clarke recorded deed 26 April 1773 from Jacob Good for £4, lot #67 in Taneytown. Eleanor wife of Jacob Good released dower.

S:186-189. Mathias Nace recorded deed 21 April 1773 from Wendel Potts, for £200, part of *Brother's Agreement.* Maudeline Potts released dower.

S:189-192. Adam Hope recorded deed 24 April 1773 from Samuel Owings Jr. for £300, tract *Norris ___,* Deborah Owings released dower rights.

S:192-195. Conrad Boner, taylor, recorded deed 26 April 1773 from Jacob Good for town lot in Taney Town. Eleanor Good released dower right.

S:195-198. George Turnball recorded deed 26 April 1773 from Jacob Good for £23, sells town lot in Taney Town. Eleanor Good released dower right.

S:198-200. Adam Good recorded deed 26 April 1773 from Jacob Good for £5..1, sells town lot in Taney Town. Eleanor Good released dower right.

S:201-204. George Will recorded deed 26 April 1773 from John Logsdon for £35..15, tract called *Amendment,* part of *Logsdon's Amendment,* containing 75 acres. Margaret Logsdon released dower rights.

S:204-206. Jacob Good recorded deed 26 April 1773 from George Baker for £5, part of *Resurvey on Brother's Agreement,* adjacent to TaneyTown, sold to Baker from Raphael Taney. Mary wife of George Baker released dower rights.

S:206. Joshua Cecill recorded assignment of mortgage 26 April 1773 from Elizabeth Dorsey for £8. Signed before Ann Beall, Bruce Worthington.

S:207. Thos Contee and John Hanson recorded bill of sale 4 May 1773 from George Walker for £20 sells bay horse, feather bed and furniture, etc. Witness: Richard Douglas.

S:208-209. Benj. Dulaney of Frederick County, Daniel Dulaney and Daniel Dulaney Jr., recorded bond for £1000, for performance of duties of Clerk of Court, 2 May 1773 from the Right Hon the Lord Proprietory. Signed before James Marshall, B. Johnson.

S:209-210. Benj. Dulaney recorded commission as clerk of the court from Henry Harford, Lord Proprietor of Maryland. Given 29 April 1773.

S:211-213. David Moore recorded deed 4 May 1773 from James McMichael, for £22..15, part of *Park Hall,* on south draft of Little Pipe Creek, 45 acres. Signed before Upton Sheriden, John McMichael. Priscilla McMichael released dower rights.

S:213-215. Alexander McGee recorded deed 4 May 1773 from John Bail, for £89, tract called *Honey Hollow,* taken up by Nicholas White, south of *Arnold's Chance.* 31 acres. Elizabeth Bail released dower.

S:216-220. Humphrey Peddicord recorded deed 4 May 1773 from Jno Bean and Daniel Weaver. Whereas Elsworth Beane by deed 6 Dec. 1760 sold to John Beane, part of *Silent Valley,* and John Bean's patent to *Bayne's Good Luck,* for 120 acres, beginning at Doc Branch, running into Bennett Creek. Assigns 100 acres.

S:220-222. William Beall of Nin. recorded release of mortgage 4 May 1773 from Thos. O. Williams and James Beall, trustees for land of William Williams deceased for £200 sells 250 acres. Signed by James Beall, son of Ninian, Thomas Owen Williams and William Beall. S:222. Jacob Linebough recorded release of dower 23 June 1773 from Elizabeth Brooke, wife of Thomas Brooke.

S:223-226. Edward Burgess and Mary, his wife recorded deed 19 May 1773 from Sarah Davis of Anne Arundel Co., spinster. Whereas Richard Snowden, ironmaster, by deed dated 3 Feb. 1749 for £111 sterling, confirmed to Sarah Davis and Mary Davis, now Mary Burgess, tract called *Snowden's Addition to his Manor,* for 555 acres, recorded in EVN12, folio 41 & 42 in the Provincial Court Records, they now divide property. M&B given, adjoins southernmost corner of Weaver Barnes land, then straight line to strike 30 perches on the 2nd line of tract containing 277 acres.

S:226-229. Joseph Warrenfelt recorded deed 4 May 1773 from Nicholas Woolf for £54 Penn. Tract, *Wolf's [Delight],* granted Nicholas Wolf in 1759. Christiana Wolf released dower rights.

S:229-231. Thomas Sims recorded bill of sale 13 May 1773 from Henry Unsel for £84 crops of wheat and rye growing on land formerly belonging to Jno Walling, but now the property of Dan'l and Samuel Hughes. Signed German Script.

S:231-233. David Stewart recorded deed 19 May 1773 from George Stewart of Annapolis, for the natural love he has for his son David and 5 shillings, assigns tract on west side of Little Conococheague containing 50 acres.

S:233-235. David Steuart recorded deed 19 May 1773 from Reverdy Ghiselin of the City of Annapolis, for 5 shillings, tract *Vexture.*

S:235-237. Nicholas Smith recorded deed 24 May 1773 from Daniel Dulaney and Walter Dulaney, executors of Daniel Dulaney, for £46..14.

S:237-240. Stephen McCloskey recorded deed 20 May 1773 from Jonathan Hager, lot #94 in Elizabeth Town. Signed before David Lynn, Samuel Beall Jr.

S:240-242. Jacob Ambrose recorded deed 24 May 1773 from George Weaver for £24, tract called *Charming Beauty,* originally granted to Jacob Weast 25 acres. Elizabeth wife of George Weaver released dower rights.

S:242-244. Peter Beard recorded deed 24 May 1773 from Charles Beatty of Frederick Town, merchant, tract called *George's Guess,* 14 ½ acres on Flemings Run; also lot in Georgetown, beginning at a corner of *Resurvey on Andrews Chance,* 13 3/4 acres. Martha Beatty released dower rights.

S:244-247. Charles Beatty and Wm Deakins recorded deed 24 May 1773 from Angus McDonald and Ann, his wife. For £50 Virginia, part of tract *Frogland,* 11 1/4 acres. Signed before Evan Shelby, John Stull.

S:247-250. David Griffith recorded deed 24 May 1773 from Jacob Good for £14, lot #20 in Taney Town. Eleanor Good released dower rights.

S:250-253. Alexander Perry recorded deed 24 May 1773 from Gerard Hopkins Jr. For £70. 5 tract *None Left,* 100 acres. Signed before Daniel of St. Thomas Jennifer, R. Ridgely. Ann wife of Gerrard Hopkins released dower.

S:253-255. Daniel Locker, taylor, recorded deed 24 May 1773 from John Margret for £12 two lots #177 & 178, in Addition to Frederick Town. Signed before Thos Price, Wm Beatty. Margaret, wife of John Margret released dower rights.

S:255-257. Michael Wine recorded deed 24 May 1773 from Chistopher Steel for 5 shillings, sells part of *Resurvey on Joseph's Friendship,* 249 acres. Catherine Steel released dower.

S:257-260. Peter & Harmon Cooling recorded deed 24 May 1773 from Yost Myers & Mary, his wife for £650, part of *Resurvey on part of Good Luck,* adjacent to *Four and a Half Gallons of Rum.*

S:261-264. Philip Hubbard recorded deed 24 May 1773 from Samuel Owings Jr. of Baltimore County, land on Deep Run, a draft of Pipe Creek for 89 acres. Deborah Owings released dower.

S:264-267. Adam Staum recorded deed 24 May 1773, from Samuel Owings Jr. of Baltimore County, for £22..10, part of tract *Ohio,* containing 50 acres. Deborah Owings released dower.

S:267-270. John Bowers recorded deed 24 May 1773 from Samuel Owings Jr. of Baltimore County, for £18..15, part of *Owing's Chance,* containing 50 acres. Deborah Owings released dower.

S:270-274. George Wilkes recorded deed 24 May 1773 from Samuel Owings Jr. of Baltimore County, for £20, part of tract *Ohio,* containing 50 acres. Signed before John Worthington, Thomas Hammond. Deborah Owings released dower.

S:274-278. Michael Turner recorded deed 24 May 1773, from Samuel Owings Jr of Baltimore County, for £25 part of tract *Ohio,* containing 50 acres. Deborah Owings released dower.

S:278-281. George Hack recorded deed 22 March 1773 from Samuel Owings Jr. of Baltimore County, for £25 part of tract *Ohio,* containing 50 acres. Deborah Owings released dower.

S:281-284. Rudolph Bruebach recorded deed 24 May 1773 from Samuel Owings Jr. of Baltimore County,for £37..2, part of *Ohio,* beginning at line of *High Germany,* containing 53 acres. Deborah Owings released dower.

S:285-288. Charles Angell recorded deed 24 May 1773 from Samuel Owings Jr. of Baltimore County, for £5 sterling, for 1st part beginning at 100 perch line of *Fryer's Delight,* 50 acres;

and 2 part beginning at bounded tre ₙₐe of *Good Hope,* for 50 acres. Deborah Owings released dower.

S:288-292. Michael McGuire recorded deed 24 May 1773 from Samuel Owings Jr of Baltimore County, for £5 sterling, part of *Ohio.* Deborah Owings released dower.

S:292-296. Jacob Fraser recorded deed 22 May 1773 from Samuel Owings Jr. of Baltimore County for £40 sells part of *Ohio,* beginning at last line of *High Germany,* 50 acres, and for 2ₙₐ part, also adjacent to *High Germany,* 100 acres. Deborah Owings released dower.

S:296-299. Michael McGuire, Jr. recorded deed 24 May 2773 from Samuel Owings Jr. of Baltimore County for £10 sterling, part of tract *Ohio,* 200 acres. Deborah Owings released dower.

S:299-303. Jacob Bankard recorded deed 24 May 1773 from Samuel Owings Jr. of Baltimore County, for £27..10 sterling, part of *Ohio,* M&B for 439 acres, and 2ₙₐ part beginning at 6ₜₕ line of *Carolina,* containing 16 acres. Deborah Owings released dower.

S:303-306. Samuel Cookson recorded deed 24 May 1773 from Leonard Kitzmiller for £150 tract *No Spring,* beginning at draft of Pipe Creek, on line of tract *Something,* taken up by Charles Carroll, 150 acres. Signed before Jos Wood, Rachel Wood. Hannah Kitzmiller released dower.

S:306-208. Robert Peter recorded deed 24 May 1773 from Alexander Offutt, for £60 part of *Clewerwell Enlarged,* M&B for 152 ½ acres, and second part of 28 acres. Signed before Will Deakins, Adam Stewart. Rebecka, wife of Alexander, released dower. AF paid William Murdock Beall.

S:308-309. Peter Smith recorded deed 24 May 1773 from Joseph, John and Andrew Rench for £200 lot #46 in Frederick Town. Signed Joseph Rentch, John Rentch, Andrew Rentch, before Wm Baird, John Stull. Margaret Rentch, widow of Peter Rentch, the former owner, released dower rights.

S:309-311. Jacob Feazer recorded deed 24 May 1773 from Charles Carroll of Annapolis, for £25, tract, *High Germany,* M&B for 50 acres.

S:311-313. James Allison recorded deed 24 May 1773 from William Frame for £33..15, tract called *Good Luck,* signed William Fream.

S:313-315. Thomas Fream recorded deed 24 May 1773 from William Fream, carpenter, for £30 part of parcel called *Good Luck,* laid out for 50 acres. Signed before Wm Blair, John McWilliams.

S:315-317. Martin Steuter recorded deed 24 May 1773 from Charles Carroll of Annapolis, for £60 assigns part of tract, *High Germany.*

S:317-319. George Zimmerman recorded deed 24 March 1773 from John Marquardt for £20 assigns two lots, #177 & 178 in Frederick Town. Mary Marquart released dower rights.

S:319-321. Joseph Wood Jr. Recorded deed 24 May 1773 from Charles Carroll for £23..17 part of *Bear Den,* 155 acres.

S:322-324. Leonard Wayman recorded deed 24 May 1773 from Gerard Hopkins Jr. of Anne Arundel County, for £90, part of *None Left,* 120 acres. Ann Hopkins released dower right.

S:324-327. Rudy Switzer recorded deed 24 May 1773 from Jacob Crumbacker for £250, part of tract lying on Little Pipe Creek, purchased by Andrew Stiger of Baltimore County, from Michael Myers by indenture 28 June 1761, recorded in Frederick County, being part of three tracts, viz *Myers Pleasure*, *Black Oak Hill* and *Marshalls Fancy*, and now called *Indian Spring*. Signed in German Script. The wife of Jacob Crumbacher, examined apart (and not named) released dower right.

S:327-329. Henry Coontz (Koonce) recorded deed 24 May 1773 from Charles Carroll of Annapolis, for £20..2 part of *Young Blood's Choice*, and part of *High Germany*. 24 acres.

S:329-332. Joseph Wood recorded deed 24 May 1773 from John Beyer, son and heir of Paul Beyer of Frederick County, turner, for £250 tract called *Parent's Lot*, being a part of tract called *The Resurvey on Good Neighborhood*, conveyed by Richard Reynolds to Paul Beyer, containing 304 acres. Margaret, wife of John Beyer, released dower.

S:332-334. James Doull recorded deed 24 May 1773 from Alexander Offutt for £40 sells part of *Clewerwell Enlarged*, M&B for 100 acres. Rebecca, wife of Alexander released dower.

S:334-337. Jacob Crumbacker recorded deed 24 May 1773 from Andrew Stiger of Baltimore County, for £180, tract beginning at *Marshall's Fancy*, adjacent to *Resurvey on Black Oak Hill*, containing 135 acres. Mary, wife of Andrew released dower.

S:338-340. Rudolph Switzer recorded deed 24 May 1773, from Andrew Stiger of Baltimore County for £108, tract puchased from Michael Myers 18 June 1761 and conveyed on 12 Dec. 1767 by Stiger to said Switzer. Mary Stiger released dower.

S:341-343. Philip Fishburn recorded deed 24 May 1773 from Christian Kinser, carpenter for £25 Penn., lot #11 in Taneytown. Signed by mark. Catherine Kinser released dower.

S:343-345. John Crumbaker recorded deed 26 April 1773 from Jacob Myer for £23, tract called *Michael's Fancy*, on draught of Little Pipe Creek for 10 acres. Signed before Upton Sheridine, Stephen Mockbee.

S:346-347. Thomas Maynard recorded deed 24 May 1773 from Ezra Beatty for £90 *Patrick's Lott*, on east bank of Linganore Creek, 2 miles below the wagon road from Monocacy to Annapolis, 90 acres. Signed before William Ricky, Benj. Maynard.

S:347-349. Henry Zeiler recorded deed 24 May 1773 from Henry Shover, blacksmith, for £250 lot #87 in Frederick Town. Signed German Script (Henrich Shuber) Anna Shover released dower.

S:349-352. Christian Kepler recorded deed 24 May 1773 from Francis Deakins, William Deakins, Jr., Daniel Hughes and Samuel Hughes for £280, part of *Resurvey on Burket's Lot*, on north side of Sexton's Branch, 223 acres. Deed acknowledged by four parties, and Rebecca, wife of Daniel Hughes released dower.

S:352-355. Philip Fishburn recorded deed 24 May 1773 from John Logsdon for £109, part of *Resurvey on Logsdon's Amendment*, 102 acres. Margaret Logsdon released dower.
S:355-357. John Crumbacker recorded deed 24 May 1773 from Jacob Crumbacker for £180, tracts *Jacob's Pasture* and *Haunces Branch*, beginning on tract called *Resurvey on Lewis Forrest*, taken up by William Lewis, for 27 acres; 2nd part *Haunces Branch*, is a part of *Michael's*

Fancy, and a part of *Resurvey on Black Oak Hill,* containing 35 acres. Catherine Crumbacher released dower rights.

S:358-359. Philip Daniel Nail, weaver, recorded deed 24 May 1773 from Adam Furnie of York County, Pennsylvania, weaver, for £94..10, part of *Carolina,* 50 acres. Barbara, wife of Adam Furnie released dower.

S:360-362. Paul Chrisman recorded deed 24 May 1773 from Jacob Rohrer for £59, small parcel, a part of *Resurvey on Hager's Fancy,* and the *Second Resurvey on Hager's Fancy.* Christiana Rohrer released dower rights.

S:363-366. Joseph Alger recorded deed 26 May 1773 from Peter Helvick for £60, part of *Black Oak Land,* beginning at draught of Piney Creek, for 45 acres. Signed G.S. Maria Maudlin, wife of Peter Helwick released dower.

S:366-369. Jacob Lockman recorded deed 16 August 1773, deed made 22 June, between Jacob Linebach for £3..4 for 2 ½ acre part of *Brookes Venture.* Signed German Script, Susannah Linebach released dower.

S:369-373. Yellos Stoufer recorded deed 16 August 1773 from Jacob Lymebach (Lineboch) for £160 99 ½ acres of *Brooke's Venture,* beginning at beginning tree of *German Town,* to the beginning tree of *Stony Ridge.* Also part of a tract called *Taylor's Bodkin,* beginning at the original beginning of *Taylor's Lot.* Susannah released dower.

S:373-375. Clement and Walter Beall recorded deed 28 June 1773 from Simon Shaffer for £310, tracts *Charles and Thomas,* 71 acres, and part of *Labyrinth,* 91 acres. Susannah Shafer released dower.

S:376-377. Frederick Dern, miller, recorded deed 28 June 1773 from William Hawk for 10 shillings, tract *The Forrest,* 44 acres. Signed by mark. Mary Hawk released dower.

S:378-380. Abram Welty recorded deed 28 June 1773 from Adam Lemmon, weaver, for £13..10, tract, *The Deep,* on Sams Creek, at south line of *The Levels.* 4 acres. Signed G.S. Margaret Lemmon released dower.

S:380-383. Henry Pott (Butt) recorded deed 28 June 1773 from Emerick (Pott) Butt for £5 sells Lot #20 in Taney Town. Annamaria Pott released dower.

S:383-386. Charles Beatty recorded deed 28 June 1773 from William Ramsey for £100 *Resurvey on Beaver Dam Branch,* 64 acres, and *Dear Bought,* 40 acres. Signed by mark.

S:386-388. Mark Alexander of Baltimore Town, recorded deed 28 June 1773 from George Lemmon for £23, lot in Taney Town. Elizabeth Lemmon released dower rights.

S:389-391. George Common, blacksmith, recorded deed 28 June 1773 from Philip Booker for £20, *Green's Fancy,* 100 acres. Catherine Booker released dower.

S:391-394. Henry Wolgamott, wheelmaker, recorded deed 28 June 1773 from John Wolgamott and Mary his wife, for £20, *Amendment,* a resurvey on three tracts: *Resurvey on Batchelor's Hope, Felty's Fortune,* and *Felty's Addition,* 7 acres.

S:395-398. Anthony Deardurff recorded deed 28 June 1773 from David Weaver of Reeding Twp., York Co., Penn., for £140 *Friends Good Will,* adjacent to old path commonly called Tuckers Path, containing 80 acres.

S:398-400. Rachel Furree of Charles County, Maryland, recorded deed 28 June 1773 from Robert Peter for £80..6, Lot #62 in Georgetown. Signed before Adam Stewart, William Deakins Jr., Elizabeth Peter released dower.

S:401-404. John Hadden recorded deed 28 June 1773 from Christopher Shockey for £60, part of *Resurvey on Sarah's Delight,* adjcent to John Shockey, Joseph Nicholson, Valentine Shockey, Philip Stamburgh, and Jacob Shockey, for 183 acres. Signed German Script. Mary Shockey released dower.

S:404-407. Paul Hawke recorded deed 28 June 1773 from William Hawke for love and affection for his son, Paul, and 5 shillings, *The Forrest,* containing 100 acres. Signed by mark before Jos Wood, Thos Reynolds. Mary Hawk released dower.

S:407-409. William Ramsey recorded deed 20 June 1773 from William Elder, Jr., for £5, *Resurvey on Beaver Dam Level,* 64 acres. Signed before Wm Blair, Elizabeth Blair.

S:410-413. Nicholas Lazear recorded deed 28 June 1773 from Emerick Pott (Butt) for £40 lot near Taney Town, on part of *Resurvey on Brother's Agreement.* 10 acres. Annamariah Pott released dower.

S:413-417. Nicholas Crowley recorded deed 28 June 1773 from Enoch Frey for £150, 55 acres of *Longate Paugh,* and *Resurvey on Longatepaugh.* Ann Fry released dower rights.

S:417-419. Robert Owen recorded deed 28 June 1773 from Thomas Edmonston for £25, part of *Resurvey on Batchelor's Forest,* called *Mount Arrarat.* Mary Edmonston released dower.

S:420-423. Francis Deakins & William Deakins Jr. Recorded deed 28 June 1773 from William Bailey Jr., for £135..11..6, *Rich Land Resurveyed,* from a certain Chs Andrews, 24 July 1768, M&B for 319 acres. Susannah Bayley released dower right.

S:424-427. Adam Baur recorded deed 28 June 1773 from Peter Booker for £230..10 three tracts, one a *I Hope It is Well Done,* containing 81 acres; *Last Shift* 50 acres, and *Resurvey on Mendall,* 5 3/4 acres.including a lane of land lying between fences of Jacob Smith and William Barnaby, totalling 137 ½ acres. Catharine Booker released dower. AF paid Wm Murdoch Beall.

S:428-431, 433-436. Casper Devilbiss recorded deed 28 June 1773 from John Kittinger for £150, *The Resurvey on Poplar Bottom,* 85 acres; part of tract called *Stouders Lookout,* 65 acres; and a tract called *Benjamin's Chores,* 13 ½ acres. However is sums paid with legal interest by John Kittinger, then this deed of bargain and sale shall be of no effect, and void. John Gittinger signed before Thos Price, Wm Beatty. Receipt. Acknowledgement.

S432 missing on film. Appears to be numbering problem in book.

S:436-439. James Coffee recorded deed 28 June 1773 from John Belt for £40 part of *Moneysworth,* at 3 line of *Warfield's Vineyard.* 158 3/4 acres. rd Jane Belt released dower. Witnesses: David Lynn, Charles Jones. AF paid Wm M. Beall.

S:440 Conrad Boner recorded release of mortgage 27 July 1773 from Philip Fishburn and Jacob Good for house & lot #4 in Taneytown.
END OF LIBER S

LIBER T
T:1-5. George Swingly recorded bill of sale 28 June 1773, from Michael Kirkpatrick for £300, *John's Lot,* on Antietam Creek, below John Stull's mill, and *Dickson's Pleasure,* on the road from Michael Waren's plantation to the mill. 63 acres. Signed before David Lynn, Aeneas Campbell. Sarah Kirkpatrick released dower.

T:5-8. Henry Riddle of PGC recorded deed 28 June 1773 from Robert Peter, merchant, tract *Long Look't For,* conveyed to him as attorney for John Glassford & Co. In consideration of a debt of Hugh Riley, at a draught of Potomac River, containing 46 acres. Signed before Andrew Heugh, Adam Stewart.

T:8-12. Christian Haas of Lancaster Co., Pa., recorded deed 28 June 1773 from Adam Welty for £200, two tracts on Sam's Creek, a draught of Little Pipe Creek, part of *Laurel Glade,* and *The Deeps,* 90 acres, & 10 acres. Signed in German script. Magdalena Welty released dower.

T:12-15. Nicholas Lazear recorded deed 28 June 1773 from Emerick Butt for £60, lot #16 in Taney Town. Signed G.S. Annamaria released dower rights.

T:16-18. John Gittings recorded deed 28 June 1773 from Christian Stouder for £150, *Resurvey on Poplar Bottom,* 85 acres; *Benjamin's Choice,* 13 ½ acres and *Stouder's Lot,* 65 acres. Barbara Stouder released dower.

T:19-22. Peter Booker recorded deeds 28 June 1773 from Bartholomew Booker, for £50, parts of *Well Done,* 87 ½ acres. adjacent to Jacob Smith. Margaret Booker, wife of Bartholomew released dower.

T:22-25. Henry Riddle of Prince George's County, merchant, recorded deed 28 June 1773, from Robert Peter for 5 shillings, tract conveyed to him as attorney for John Glassford & Co. From Joseph Hughes, for a debt by Timothy Whitehead, 35 acres.

T:25-38. Martin Shoup recorded deed 28 June 1773 from Jacob Knouf for £184..10, *The Legacy,* 100 acres. Elizabeth, wife of Jacob Knave released dower.

T:28-30. John Carn (Karn) recorded deed 28 June 1773 from John Smay for £30, tract on north side of Kitoctin Mountain, 3/4 miles from Jacob Knave's plantation, containing 50 acres. Signed in G.S. Susanna, wife of John Smay released dower.

T:31-33. Jonathan Fry recorded deed 28 June 1773 from Enoch Fry. Refers to previous deed for *Longatepaugh,* recorded in Liber P. 50 acres.

T:33-35. William Hawke recorded deed 28 June 1773 from Charles Carroll for £88, part of *Forrest* on Great Pipe Creek. 144 acres.

T:36-38. Jacob Good recorded deed 28 June 1773 George Lemmon for £100, *Resurvey on Brothers Agreement,* 3 acres. Elizabeth Lemmon released dower.

T:39-41. George Breackley recorded deed 28 June 1773 from Philip Booker for £20, *Well Done,* 72 acres. Catherine wife of Philip released dower.

T:41-44. Joseph Talbott recorded deed 28 June 1773 from Henry Hall for £161..6..8, for *Henry and Elizabeth,* 504 acres.

T:44-45. Henry Wade & Richard Wade recorded agreement from Joseph Kitcham to let them build a house on a small place of ground near the beginning of Henry Barnes, lot #17, to extend toward Joshua Davis, during said Kitcham's continuance on said lease, Henry and Richard to pay rents.

T:45-48. Ambrose Cook recorded bill of sale 28 June 1773 from John Mummert for £60..2, part of *Robert's Choice,* 59 acres, and one other tract, *Mummert's Choice,* 11 acres.

T:48 Marian Walter recorded certificate (of survey) 22 July 1773 from Marian Richardson. Whereas Marian Richardson, deceased, by will and testament bequeath 100 acres of part of *Addition to Brooke Grove,* which Richardson purchased from Thomas Snowden, and laid out in survey 21 March 1769. Plat included.

T:49-51. John Leidy recorded deed 23 July 1773 from Jacob Hose, joyner, for £20 lot #81 in Elizabeth Town. Molly Hose, wife of Jacob Hose released dower.

T:51-53. Jacob Peck, weaver, Jacob Peck, smith, and Anthony Nobel, recorded bill of sale 27 July 1773 from James Graham, for £11..14..1, in consideration of their entering for his appearance at the suit of Peter Becraft and Jacob Upright, all his crops of wheat and Indian Corn. Signed by mark before Francis Adams, David Meek.

T:53-58. Chrstopher King recoreded deed 16 Aug. 1773 from Andrew Simpson for £272..10, tract *Scott Comfort,* adjacent to *Charlton's Victory,* for 143 acres. Angus Sympson wife of Andrew released dower.

T:58-62. William Harris of Baltimore County, recorded deed 16 Aug. 1773 from Conrad Boner, taylor. Whereas a former grant by John Hoover of York County, Penn., for lot #4, Taney Town, did not include convents, and payments due to Ralph Taney.

T:62-64. William Reynolds recorded deed 16 August 1773 from John Brown for £200, part of *Resurvey on Brooke's Resurvey,* made by John McMahan to John Brown. Elizabeth Brown released dower.

T:65-67. Robt Isidor recorded deed 16 Aug. 1773 from John Barrick for £160, lot #87 in Sharpsburgh Town. Signed in German Script, Johannes Borg. Ann Margaret Barrick released dower.

T:67-68. Robt Isidor recorded deed 16 Aug. 1773 from John Barrick for £140, lot #32 in Sharpsburgh Town. Signed in German Script, Johannes Borg. Ann Margaret Barrick released dower.

T:69-73. Jacob Zeller recorded deed 16 August 1773 from John Yager for £200, tract, *Resurvey on Egypt,* 58 acres. Barbara Yager released dower.

T:74-76. Jacob Weller recorded deed 16 August 1773 from Jacob Linebough, for £27 tract originally granted him by Thomas Brook, *Vine Garden,* on Broad Run, a draught of Great Hunting Creek, 27 acres. Susanna Linebough released dower.

T:76-78. Nicholas Elvesta (Helvesta) recorded deed 16 August 1773 from Peter Yeater for £9 *Phillip's Chance,* on Little Antietam, 15 acres. Signed GS. Wife, not named, released dower.

T:79-83. Jacob Harbough recorded deed 16 Aug. 1773 from John Penrad for £400 for three tracts, *Hone's Foot,* at foot of hill near *Pleasant Level* containing 16 acres; *Resurvey on Zealand,* 383 acres and tract called *Good Bunch,* resurvey on *Mount Olive, Sweedland and Tied Dog,* 18 acres. Signed by mark before Wm Blair, and Patrick Alexander. Catherine Penrad released dower.

T:84-85. Jacob Wolf recorded deed 19 Aug. 1773 from Joseph Chapline for £6, lot #84 in Sharpsburgh.

T:86-87 Jacob Wolf recorded deed 19 Aug. 1773 from Joseph Chapline for £6..10, lot #83 in Sharpsburgh.

T:88-92. James Hill recorded lease 19 Aug. 1773 from John Chisholm, schoolmaster, tract, *Jedburgh Forrest,* 67 acres, for term of 20 years, for rents and to plant 50 apple trees. Signed by both before Thomas Reynolds by mark and Mary Stewart.

T:92-T96. Charles Jones recorded deed of confirmation 19 Aug. 1773 from Edward Beall of Alexander, deceased, and Archibald Beall and Jane, his wife. Whereas in 1759 William Beall and Jane Edmonston sold part of *Labyrinth,* to Charles Jones, adjacent to *Clagett's Purchase,* deed to correct mistake. Rachel Beall wife of Edward Beall released dower right before David Lynn, Edward Burgess.

T:96-100. Thomas Welsh recorded deed 21 August 1773 from John Buchanan, of London, merchant. Whereas, James Wardrop of Prince George's County, merchant, now deceased, by indenture of lease and release, 2 August 1754, granted John Buchanan, tract called *Brentford,* originally granted James Wardrop in 9 August 1750. Since death of said Wardrop, sold at public vendue to highest bidder for £30, for 35 acres. Mr. John Buchanan appointed Judson Coolidge his attorney for sale. Signed before J. Hepburn.

T:100-102. John Brown and John Collins recorded lease 21 Aug. 1773 from Jacob Shea, miller, part of tract called *Poplar Bottom,* containing by estimation 125 acres, for term of 5 years. Signed by all three parties.

T:102-103. Martha Tucker recorded deed of gift 21 August 1773 from Isaac Stallings in consideration of natural love and affection for my daughter, and 5 shillings, grants during her natural life one Negro girl named Tamar, and at the death of my daughter, to her daughter Kathrine Tucker, and to her heirs, and her issue to be divided between Katherine Tucker and Susanna Tucker. Signed by mark before Andrew Hugh and Henry Wilson of Lancelot.

T:104-108. Daniel Culp, tanner, and Balser Gall, merchant recorded deed 21 Aug. 1773 from Jacob Petry of Elizabeth Town, miller, for £57..10 lot in Elizabeth Town. Eve Petry released dower rights.

T:108-110. George Bond Sr. recorded land commission 23 Aug. 1773 on the *Forrest*, petitioned court before Thomas Prather and his associates, to examine evidence to perpetuate the bounds. Issued 19 Feb. 1772. Followed by deposition of John Darling, sworn, that he saw small black oak, close by a draught which lay across the lane between the said land and Peter Hoover's, about 100 yards from the spring of said land. He carried the chain when the survey was run on the tract.

T:110-113. Henry Shaw recorded mortgage 23 August 1773 from John Gomp for £14 lot in Additional Lots to Frederick Town, #249. Signed John Comb.

T:113-117. Henry Ready recorded 24 August 1773, from Jacob Storm, for £160 tract called *Storm's Lott,* part of the *Resurvey on Antietam Bottom,* 25 acres and one other tract. Margaret Storm released dower.

T:117-119. Normand Bruce recorded bill of sale 12 Sep 1773 from Robert Watson for £31 sells livestock Signed by mark.

T:119-121. Joshua Ragan recorded deed 23 Aug. 1773 from Doctor James Brand for £16, lot in Additional lotts to Frederick Town, #168. Acknowledgment. AF paid Wm M Beall.

T:122-125. Cornelius Carmack recorded deed 23 Aug. 1773 from Jacob Myers, carpenter, for £320 parts of several tracts, *Resurvey on Lewis Forrest,* Resurvey called *Michl Taney,* and Resurvey called *Black Oak Hill,* beginning at beginning tree of tract called *Level Spring,* 150 acres more or less.

T:125-127. George Bowers recorded deed 23 Aug. 1773 from John Lyde for one shilling, lot #120 in Jerusalemtown. Julany wife of John Lyde released dower.

T:128-130. John Gomp (or Comb) recorded deed 23 August 1773 from Anthony Boley for £14, lot #249 in Additional Lots to Frederick Town. Signed G.S. Margaret Boley released dower.

T:130-133. Michael Hoover recorded deed 23 Aug. 1773 from Abraham Hull for £25 parcel called *Spear,* at the foot of South Mountain, containing 30 acres. Elizabeth Hull released dower.

T:133-136. Melchor Beltzhoover recorded deed 23 Aug. 1773 from Jona Hagar for £10 lot #85 in Elizabeth Town, where he now lives. Signed before Wm Baird, John Stull.

T:136-139. James Suter, taylor, recorded deed 9 May 1773 from William Haymond, joiner, for £212..10, *Constant Friendship,* 150 acres. Signed before David Lynn, T. Sprigg Wootton. Cassandra Haymond released dower rights.

T:139-142. John McAllister, storekeeper, recorded deed 24 May 1773, from Ths Stevenson, for £900 part of *Frenchman's Purchase,* patented by Col. Samuel Beall, beginning at Jas Morrison's part of said tract, for 500 acres.

T:142-144. James Chapline recorded deed 2 May 1773 from William Williams Chapline, for natural love and affection he has for his brother and £20, assigns *Resurvey on Hills and Dales,* and *Vinyard,* on west side of Big Antietam, also my mill on Little Antietam, and one other tract, *Resurvey on Vinyard.*

T:145-146. Walter Beall recorded bill of sale 4 May 1773 from Simon Sheffer. [marginal note: examined and delivered Thaddeus Beall]. For £150 assigns crop of corn nowgrowing, one lot of blacksmith's tools, one bay mare, other horses, cattle enumerated; one servant man, William McCoy; servant woman, Jane McCoy and servant girl, Catherine McCoy, and one knife. Nevertheless if sum paid, sale is void. Deliver of one knife sealed sale.

T:147-150. George Swingle recorded deed 4 May 1773, from Michael Kirkpatrick. Whereas George Swingle did agree for 100 acres of land, to build and erect a mill on tract called *John's Lot,* and part of *Dickson's Pleasure,* for £300 and the privilege of raising and building a dam on part of *John's Lott,* across Big Antietam, the aforesaid Michael Kirkpatrict is also to have privilege of setting a fish pot between the tail race and the mill dam.

T:151-153. Ludwig Lawman and John Hubley of the "Burrow" of Lancaster, Lancaster Co., Penn., recorded deed 19 Nov. 1773 from Dr. Thomas Polhouse of Frederick Town, for £169..9, sells lots in Frederick Town, formerly belonging to Joseph Hardman, deceased, parts of lots 199, 200, 201, 202, 204, 205, 206 and #235.

T:154-156. George Shultz Jr. Recorded deed 24 May 1773 from Peter Whitestone for £30, Pennsylvania. [marginal note: Delivered Normand Bruce, 30 Nov. 1787]. Part of a tract in Conecocheague settlement. Called *Hazard,* alias *Conquest,* 33 acres.

T:156-159. George Shultz Jr. Recorded deed 24 May 1773 from Peter Whetstone for £50, part of tract called *Resurvey on Hortman's Place,* in Conococheague Settlement, containing 25 acres.

T:159-161. Joseph Chapline recorded deed 24 May 1773 from Benjamin Ogle of the City of Annapolis, for £300, *Resurvey on Vinyard,* 503 acres. Appointed Richard Davis of Frederick County, attorney. Signed before Dan'l of St. Thos Jenifer, Richard Sprigg. Henry Margaret, wife of Benjamin Ogle released dower rights.

T:161-163. Sarah Shaw recorded deed from Benjamin Ogle Junr. of Frederick County,. Whereas the said Sarah Shaw, then Sarah Henry, on 16 June 1772, sold tracts *Ogleton* and *Kingstonstead,* 150 acres plus 50 acre part. See Liber P:239-241. Benjamin Ogle Jr. Signed before Charles Jones, Edward Burgess.

T:164-166. Michael Kirkpatrick recorded deed 24 May 1773 from Daniel Dulaney and Walter Dulaney, executors of Daniel Dulaney, deceased late of Annapolis, for £56..6..4, tract called *John's Lot.*

T:166-167. John Glassford & Co recorded bill of sale 18 June 1773 from Robert Peters for £30 sterling, paid to me by James Duley, the price of a Negro girl, Sarah, sold to him by a certain Joseph Beall, which was mortgaged to John Glassford, and assigned rights to the following three Negroes, Cupic, Peter and Sun, and the increase of Sun since 1758 the day they were sold to me by the within Joseph Bell. Signed Robert Peter before Adam Stewart, John Dunlop.

T:167-170. Henry Hime recorded lease 31 May 1773 from Samuel Chew and Bennett Chew of Anne Arundel County, for rents and covenants herein, leases for 21 years 100 acres, lot #32,, On back, is assignment of lease dated 24 April 1773 to Peter Consella, signed Henry Hime before Richard Davis, Bazil Rhoades.

T:170-172. Andrew Heugh, for Messrs Stewart & Campbell of London, merchants, and others [Clement Beall and Jonathan Nixon] recorded bill of sale 16 Aug. 1773 from William Needham for sums of £25..15 sterling; 2666 lbs crop tobacco and £18 sterling due to Jonathan Nixon and also £30..15 due by me to Clement Beall, assigns 20 head of cattle, one small mare, one sorrel mare, one black mare called Jewel, 12 head of hogs. Signed by William Needham before Charles Jones, John Dalrymple Needham.

T:173-176. Peter Redingour recorded deed 23 Aug. 1773 from Jonathan Hager and Martin Kershner, executors of Martin Kershner deceased for £10 sells parts of three tracts, *Amendment, Trouble with Contentment,* 19 ½ acres, a second part for 8 acres, and the tract *First Snow* for 22 acres.

T:176-178. Daniel Brown recorded deed 23 Aug. 1773 from Joseph Dyer for £35, tract *Dyer's Mill Forrest,* adjacent to *Long Acre,* to the part of *Mill Forrest* in possession of Rudolph Brubach, to 2 line nd of *Bills Choise.* Containing 71 acres. Joannah, wife of Joseph Dyer released dower.

T:178-181. Asher Layton recorded deed 23 Aug. 1773 from Isaac Burton for £60 sells parcel called *Hard Bargain,* a part of a tract called *Resurvey on Content,* containing 86 acres. Signed by mark before Charles Jones, Jos Wood. Sarah Burton, wife of Isaac, released dower.

T:181-184. Stephen West of Prince George's County, merchant, recorded deed 29 Sept. 1771, made 28 August 1771, from John Gordon, mariner, son of George Gordon of Prince George's County, deceased. Whereas John Gordon did heretofore, on 9 March 1768, convey to Stephen West, lot #75 near the River in Georgetown; for £126 now agrees to release all encumbrances. Signed before John Duvall, John Smith Brooks.

T:184-187. Ezra Beatty, joiner, recorded deed 23 Aug. 1773 from Thomas Beatty of Frederick County for £458, tract called *Leonard's Folly,* near a spring descending into Linganore 135 acres; also part of *Middle Plantation,* conveyed by John Hall to Thomas Beatty, to beginning tree of William Williams' land, 750 acres.

T:188-192. George Kershner recorded deed 23 Aug. 1773 from Jonathan Hager and Martin Kershner, executors of Martin Kershner, deceased, for £60 assigns part of *Resurvey on Dutch's Folly, Addition to Dutch's Folly, the Widow's Last Shift,* beginning at *Resurvey on Contentment,* laid out for 169 acres. Agreement in deed regarding use of water from spring on line of tract with John Kershner's part of lands.

T:192-195. Patrick Watson of York County, Pennsylvania, joiner, recorded deed 23 Aug 1773 from Joseph Ludshaw, for £10 sells lot #9 near Tawney Town, containing 5 acres. Maudlin, wife of Joseph Ludshaw released dower.

T:195-198. Nicholas Toup recorded deed 23 Aug. 1773, from Phillip Rodenpillar, weaver for £50, tract *Philip Rodenpiller's Ramble by Quaker Trick,* for 110 ½ acres. Rachel Rodenpiller released dower.

T:198-202. Nicholas Shover recorded deed 23 Aug. 1773 from Jonathan Hager and Martin Kershner executors of the will of Martin Kersner, deceased, for £150, sells part of *Resurvey on Batchelor's Delight,* and The *Hartman.*

T:202-204. Philip Judea recorded deed 23 Aug. 1773 from William Tucker for £15, for 15 acres on *Second Resurvey on Black Acorn.* Signed by mark. Rachel Tucker released dower.

T:204-207. Benjamin Whitmore recorded deed 23 Aug. 1773 from William Biggs for £130 tract made over to William Biggs by Benjamin Biggs 14 Nov. 1771 called *Biggs Adventure* (Liber O:651) being part of *Benjamin's Good Luck,* 96 acres. Wife of William Biggs (not named) released dower right.

T:207-210. Harmon Claphert recorded deed 23 Aug. 1773 from Jonathan Hager. Whereas by indenture made 9 Sept. 1769, and the consideration therein, assigns lot #9 in Elizabeth Town.

T:210-213. Nicholas Rouce recorded deed 23 Aug. 1773 from John Rohrer for £20, sells part of *Second Resurvey on Nancy's Content,* containing 2 1/8 acres. Nancy Rohrer released dower.

T:214-216. Michael Null recorded deed 23 Aug. 1773 from Daniel Brown for £150, *Resurvey on Brother's Agreement,* beginning at the east line of Thomas Fisher's land, containing 50 acres. Margaret, wife of Daniel Brown, released dower.

T:216-219. William Ferguson recorded deed 23 June 1773 from Henry Fullwider for £150, being part of Henry Fister's part of *Resurvey on Chevy Chase.* 60 acres. Barbara Fullwider released dower rights.

T:219-222. Jacob Crist recorded deed 23 Aug 1773 from Jacob Moiley, wagon maker, for £20 assigns part of tract *Irishewen,* patented by Archibald McNabb, containing 20 acres. Christinas wife of Jacob Moiley released dower

T:222-225. James Young of York County, Pennsyvania, recorded deed 23 August 1773 from James Cochran and Wm. Cochran, executors of William Cochran, deceased, tract *Carrollsburgh.* Whereas in his lifetime William Cochran made bond unto John Galloway of York County for 200 acres, and Galloway assigned the bond to James Young, now for £93..4 paid in his lifetime, plus £74..11..4, assigns tract.

T:225-229. Paul Rhodes recorded deed 23 August 1773 from Jacob Rhorar for £100, *Rorar's Lott,* 29 ½ acres; 2nd part, *Rhorar's Addition,* patented by Jacob Rohrer Sr., for 100 acres; laid off for 46 acres and the 3rd small part called *Resurvey on George's Mistake, George's Venture* and the *Barrens,* 33 acres. Fronica Rohrer, widow of Jacob Rohrer Sr. Released dower.

T:230-234. John Shyrock Sr., living in York Town, Pennsylvania, pump maker, recorded deed 23 August 1773 from Jacob Rohrer, for £61, part of the original resurvey on *Hager's Fancy,* 5 ½ acres. Christian Rohrer, wife to Jacob Rohrer released dower.

T:234-238. Jacob Warrenfeltz recorded deed 23 Aug 1773 from John Martin for £50, tract called *Baker's Delight,* containing 50 acres. Anna Maria, wife of John Martin released dower.

T:238-241. Joachim Strafer recorded deed 23 Aug 1773 from Adam Ream, for £85, tract called *Witman's Loss,* 40 3/4 acres. Wife of Adam Ream (not named) released dower.

T:241-244. Jacob Stover recorded deed 23 Aug. 1773, from Jacob Moiley for £60 sells 60 acre part of tract, *Irishewen,* patented to Archibald McNabb. Christiana Moiley released dower.

T:243-247. Martin Rhorar recorded deed 23 Aug. 1773, from John Rhorar for £51 sells part of *Brother's Request,* now called *Rhorar's Fancy,* containing 46 ½ acres. Nancy Rhorar, wife of John released dower.

T:247-250. Michael Fackler recorded deed 23 Aug. 1773 from Jonathan Hager for £10 Pennsylvania, lot #105 in Elizabeth Town.

T:250-253. Jacob Coughman recorded deed 23 Aug. 1773 from John Rhorer for £55, part of *John's Adventure,* originally a part of *Resurvey on Scared from Home,* for 60 acres. Nancy Rhorer, wife of the within John released dower.

T:254-256. Adam Camp recorded deed 23 Aug. 1773 from Henry Bytesell for £5, part of *Smith's Hap,* containing 1 acre and 25 perches.

T:256-258. Simon Bowman recorded deed 23 Aug. 1773 from Jonathan Hager, references earlier deed in 1768 between the two parties for lot #23 in Elizabeth Town, to correct acknowledgment of deed.

T:258-260. Moses Carr recorded deed 20 Aug. 1772 from Michael Cresap for £20 sterling, tract called *Charlie's Lott,* originally granted Charles Allanson Ford, 100 acres by patent, in 1766,

T:260-262. Charles Robinson recorded deed 23 August 1773 from Samuel Emmitt for £96 Pennsylvania, tract called *Carrolsburg,* 120 acres. Mary Emmitt released dower.

T:263-265. Enoch Frey recorded deed 23 August 1773 from John Heineke for £75, 40 acres, part of *Resurvey on Longatebough.* Barbara Heineke released dower rights.

T:265-270. Rinehart Replogle recorded deed 23 Aug. 1773 from Mathias Oatt for £550 part of *Resurvey on Smith's Lott,* to line of tract of Nathaniel Nesbitt, for 150 acres of land. Elizabeth, wife of Mathias Oatt released dower.

T:270-273. John Robinson recorded deed 23 August 1773 from Ludowick Rhine, for £90 tract called *Ludwick's Lott,* on west side of Toms Creek, near Monocacy, 26 acres. The second tract being part of a resurvey called *Carolina,* being confirmed and made over to him by Benedict Calvert, Normand Bruce, Edward Diggs and William Diggs by deed of sale 4 June 1767 in Liber K:1427-1428. Mary, wife of Ludwick Rhine released dower.

T:273-275. Philip Erhard recorded deed 23 August 1773 from Edward Rutter for £300 tract called *Gaming Alley,* on south side of the Great Road that leads from Stulls Mill to Monocacy, and near the end of a tract called *Rutter's Delight,* containing 100 acres. Mary Rutter released dower.

T:275-279. Jacob Rhorar recorded deed 23 August 1773, from Fronica Rhorar for £200 sells *Resurvey on Stoney Corner,* 83 acres. *Resurvey on French's Lot,* beginning at a resurvey on the following tracts: *George's Venture, Barrens and George's Mistake,* containing 58 acres. Signed by mark.

T:279-281. Francis Mantz recorded deed 23 Aug. 1773 from Elenor Charlton of Frederick Town, executrix of Arthur Charlton late of Frederick County, deceased, by his will ordered that his lots within Frederick Town be sold and the money to be divided among his children. Purchased by Thomas Mantz for £44..5 three lots.

T:282-283. Edward Snickers recorded power of attorney 4 Feb 1774 from Humphrey Wells of Georgia, Parish of St. Paul. There was a constract some years ago between Solomon Wright of Queen Anne County, lawyer, and said Humprhey about some land I sold in Queen Anne County, by bond of conveyance, and I relying on the honesty of Edwd Snickers of Frederick

County, Virginia, have appointed him lawful attorney to act in my name to convey land to the said Solomon Wright. Signed Humphrey Wells before Dan Morgan, Elijah Isaacs.

T:283-285. Richard Butler recorded deed 23 August 1773 from Daniel Dulaney. Whereas on 15 June 1751, Daniel Dulaney Esq., deceased father of the said Daniel Dulaney part hereto, received from Frederick Vertrees, then of Frederick Town, the full, for a lot in Frederick Town, which he improved and which said lot the said Daniel Dulaney deceased by writing agreed to convey to the said Frederick Vertrees, and also two other lots, upon paying £2..4..6. Afterwards in 1752, Peter Butler, deceased, father of the said Richard Butler, his heir, obtained condemnation for two lots in Frederick Town, #95 and 96, as the property of Frederick Vertrees, being the same lots agreed to be conveyed on payment; and the said Peter Butler by his will, bequeath this two part of it should be paid to his wife Mary, and the rest among his children; but the said £2 was never paid. Now for consideration of rents and covenants hereinafter mentioned, assigns to Richard Butler for £10..8..8 and the £2..4..6 and legal interest thereon, the aforesaid two lots, #95 and #96.

T:285-287. Peter Hooze, carpenter, recorded deed 23 Aug. 1773 from Jonathan Hager, for £8, sells ½ of lot #127 in Elizabeth Town. Signed before John Stull, Wm Baird. Alienation fine paid Wm M Beall.

T:287-289. Christopher Alden recorded deed 23 August 1773 from Jonathan Hager, for £8, sells one half of lot #127 in Elizabeth Town.

T:290-292. Frederick Shultz recorded deed from John Youst Owenbride. [Marginal note, delivered to Jacob Harbaugh, 5 March 1784, to be as attorney for grantee.] Said John Youst Ownprade for 24 shillings, confirms to Frederick Shultz 25 acres of land in Frederick County, called *Bucks Horn.* Mary, wife of John Youstownprade released dower.

T:292-293. Edmond Rutter recorded deed 23 August 1773, from Phillip Erhart for £200 lot #9 in Frederick Town. Signed Philip Arhart. Mary, wife of Philip released dower.

T:294-296. Jacob Shuh, miller, recorded deed 23 Aug. 1773, from Christian Stouder for £300 sells 125 acres, part of *Resurvey on Pawpaw Bottom,* laid out for 125 acres. Barbara wife of Christian released dower.

T:296-298. John Fletchall recorded deed 23 Aug. 1773 from John Flint, carpenter, for £66..5, part of tract *Flint's Grove,* for 50 acres.

T:298-300. Jacob Blessing recorded deed 27 Aug. 1773 from Christiana Blessing, widow, for £18 sells her right of dower to tract formerly possessed by her husband, Nicholas Blessing, deceased, called *Brother's Good Will.* 200 acres. Signed by mark.

T:300-303. Patrick Watson of York County, Pennsylvania, recorded deed 23 Aug 1773 from Joseph Ludshaw of Taney Town, for £60 lot #6, on the main road, leading from Frederick Town to York Town. Maudlin, wife of Joseph Ludshaw released dower.

T:303-306. Robt Peter and Adam Stewart, merchants, recorded deed 23 Aug. 1773 from James White Senr. Of Prince George's County, for £625, assigns parcels in Frederick County on or near Rock Creek, called *Mill Seat,* and part of *Good Luck,* the condemned land being part of the original tract *Addition to Fellowship,* and part of *New Addition,* which land adjoins each other, in the whole included in metes and bounds given, to a line of *Good Luck,* at end of 6th line of Ninian Mockabee, containing 300 acres. Eleanor wife of James White released dower rights.

T:307-309. Elias Delashmutt Jr recorded deed 20 Aug. 1773 from Thomas Fee for £50 part of *Deptford,* beginning about 50 feet from a spring that falls into Kitoctin Creek, containing 32 acres. Also part of a tract called *White Oak Spring,* adjoining *Deptford,* containing 18 acres. Signed by mark. Sarah Fee, wife of Thomas, released dower rights.

T:309-312. Daniel Brown recorded deed 23 Aug. 1773 from Peter Erb Jr. for £80 sells tract called *Belt's Choice,* beginning about 66 perches NE from said Belt's house, laid out for 54 acres. Wife of Peter Erb (not named) released dower rights.

T:312-316. George Keivelor. recorded deed 23 Aug. 1773 from Jonathan Hager and Martin Kershner, executors of Martin Kershner deceased, for £100 assigns tract called *Resurvey on part of the Resurvey on Batchelor's Delight,* and part of a tract of land called the *Hartman,* 130 acres. Receipt, the sum of £100 Pennsylvania. AF paid.

T:316-318. Nicholas Martin recorded deed 23 Aug. 1773 from Henry Ridenour for £20 tract called *Resurvey on Henry's Last Shift, and Nicholas Ridenour's Pond,* for 16 ½ acres. Eve, wife of Henry released dower.

T:318-320. Ninian Clagett recorded deed of gift 23 Aug. 1773 from Thomas Clagett for 5 shillings and the natural love and affection he has for his son, tract called *Flints Grove,* metes and bounds for 100 acres.

T:320-322. William Beatty recorded deed 23 Aug. 1773 from Ezekiel Beatty for £200, one half of lot #65, in Frederick Town, that adjoins the Calvanist Church Lot, on which Benjamin Johnson now lives.

T:322-325. Daniel and Samuel Hughes recorded deed 23 Aug. 1773 from Henry Pitner for £25 part of tract called *Done in Haste,* near the Poplar Cabbin, containing 50 acres, Dorothy, wife of Henry Pitner released dower.

T:325-330. Jacob Kershner recorded deed 23 Aug. 1773 from Jonathan Hager and Martin Kersner, executors of Martin Kershner deceased, for £72 assigns tract called *Resurvey on Trouble with Contentment,* called the *Amendment,* 46 acres; then for 2nd tract, small parcel part of Resurvey on above tract called *The Amusemenmt,* for 15 acres.

T:330-332. Christopher Erb recorded deed 23 Aug 1773 from Joseph Dyer for £33, for 53 acres, part of *Dyer's Mill tract,* Signed before Joseph Wood, Charles Jones. Joannah Dyer, wife of Joseph, released dower.

T:333-338. John Kershner recorded deed 23 Aug. 1773 from Jonathan Hager and Martin Kershner, executors of Martin Kershner deceased, for £60, part of tract, *Resurvey on Dutch Folly, Addition to Dutch Folly, Widows Last Shift,* and one *Contentment,* 178 acres.

T:338 Daniel Viers recorded bill of sale 25 August 1773, from Nehemiah Veirs for £200, 9 head of cattle, another cow marked differently, together with 30 head of hogs, one servant man named George Craigg, indented with a molatto servent girl, under indenture named Hannah Mutter; one dark bay horse, one white horse, one black mare, 9 head of sheep, two feather beds, pots, pewter, chairs, tables, axes, ploughs, hoes and all moveable, with my whole crop of corn and tobacco now in growth on my plantation. Signed before Thos Price, Thos Price Junr.

T:340-343. Teter Rudy recorded deed 17 August 1773, from William Tucker for £200 sells part of *Resurvey on Black Acorn,* adjacent to Philip Judea's part, 123 acres. Rachel, wife of Wm Tucker released dower.

T:344-346. Matthias Ahalt recorded deed 3 Aug. 1773 from William Tucker for 5 shillings, assigns part of the *Second Resurvey on Black Acorn,* containing 70 acres. Rachel, wife of Wm Tucker released dower.

T:346-348. George Jacob Baltzell recorded deed 23 Aug. 1774 from William May for £30 called *May's Folly,* about 4 perches from a spring in the Shannadondore Mountains, containing 18 acres. The wife of William May (not named) released dower.

T:348-350. Henry Hunt of the Kingdom of Ireland, recorded 23 Aug. 1773 from James Spurgeon of the Province of Maryland, for £25 Pennsylvania, sells tract on main branch of Town Creek, containing 50 acres.

T:350-353. George and Jacob Baltzell recorded deed 23 Aug. 1773 from William May for £30 assigns tract called *Bad Enough,* adjacent to tract called *Much Grumbling,* containing by estimation 30 acres. At same time, wife of William May (not named) released dower.

T:353-355. Peter Shover recorded deed 23 Aug. 1773 from Jacob Ambrose for £554 grants 100 acres, adjacent to part of Henry Ambroses 268 acres of part of tract *Arnold's Delight.* Signed before David Lynn, Edward Burgess. Catherine, wife of Jacob released dower.

T:355-358. Samuel Green recorded deed 23 Aug. 1773 from Basil Lucas, innkeeper, for £52..10 tract called *Hard Struggle,* beginning at north west branch of the Eastern Branch of the Potomac, containing 52 ½ acres. Signed before Robert Peter, Adam Stewart. Amey, wife of Basil Lucas released dower.

T:358-361. Peter Erb recorded deed 23 Aug. 1773 from Joseph Dyer for £25 assigns part of *Dyer's Mill Forrest,* 50 acres more or less. Joannah, wife of Joseph released dower.

T:361-363. Samuel Green recorded deed 29 Sep 1773 from Thomas Lucas of Baltimore County, miller, assigns parts of tracts known as *Jackson's Improvement*, and part of *Friendship Inlarged,* on the north west branch, laid out for 194 acres.

T:363-365. Colin Dunlap & son, merchants, recorded bill of sale 26 Aug 1773 from Samuel Lewis Jr. for £15 one red cow, one black cow, two sows and 14 shoats, one bay horse; also my crop of tobacco in the ground and wheat in stock, one feather bed and bed cloathes and two iron pots. Signed before William Deakins Junr., William Wilson.

T:365-367. Ignatius Thompson recorded deed 26 Aug. 1773 from Benjamin Sweet for £32..10 part of tract called *Sideling Hill,* for 36 ½ acres. Signed by mark before Sam'l Beall Junr., John Stull. Martha, wife of Benjamin Sweet released dower.

T:367-369. AlexanderThomas Hawkins recorded release 8 Sept. 1773 from Nicholas Leatherman, regarding *Hawkins Merry Peep a Day,* 200 acres. During the natural lives of the aforesaid Nicholas Leatherman, Elizabeth Leatherman his wife and Christian Leatherman their son, the reversion whereof doth belong to Alexander Thomas Hawkins of Prince George's County, now know ye, that for 5 shillings, doth surrender and give up their right to the title. Signed before Wm Beall, Richd Burgess.

T:369-371. Robert Wellmore recorded lease 14 Sept. 1773 from Francis Ratliff for yearly rents and considerations, for 20 year term, land tats in a lease, possessed of Samuel Hanson, eastward of the premises, to build one tobacco house, one dwelling house, plant two orchards of 100 apple trees, and 100 peach trees, Signed Francis Ratliff.

T:371-372. James Patterson recorded bill of sale 21 Sept 1773 from Charles Chaney Junr., all the indian corn and fodder now standing in plantation, I the aforesaid Charles Cheney Junr. Have sold to Richard Donaldson, containing about 10 or 11 acres; also a red cow, and red heifer, that now goes along with Thos Powel's Senr. Cattle, for £16 Signed by mark in the presence of Alexander Falconer, Richard Donaldson.

T:372-373. Joseph Ford and William Ford (and others) recorded deed of gift 20 Sept 1773 from Ann Ford, widow. For and in consideration of the love, good will and affection I have for my children, Joseph Ford, William Ford, John Ford, Hezekiah Magruder Ford , James Ford and Samuel Ford, now living in the county aforesaid, give to them my Negro girl Kate, and her increase; after my decease. Signed by mark befoe Charles Jones, Mary Jones, Sarah Jones.

T:373. John Calhoun recorded bill of sale 12 Oct. 1773 from James Anderson of Frederick County, for £25 sells one bright bay horse, 14 ½ hands high.

T:374-376. Sampson Trammell of Virginia, recorded deed 6 Oct. 1773 from John Hopkins sells tract called *Island,* on Potomac River, formerly taken up by Walter Evans Senr., receipt for £112. Eleanor, wife of John Hopkins released dower.

T:376-378. John Bennett, miller, recorded deed 6 Oct. 1773 from Neal McFall, for £20 part of tract called *Resurvey on the Three Friends,* laid out for 5 acres.

T:379-381. Jonathan Roze recorded deed 18 May 1774, made 5 May between John Myers of Frederick City, for £277, all of the following tracts, *Resurvey on Bayleys Fancy,* 200 acres; also tract called *Meadows Pleasure,* beginning at bank of Potomac River, and the lower end of a bottom opposite to the mouth of Hoopy Creek in Virginia side, laid out for 50 acres; Catherine wife of John Myers released dower.

T:382-384. John Bennett recorded deed 6 Oct. 1773 from John Ulrich for £1600 Pennsylvania, tract called *Struggle,* being a resurvey on *Three Friends,* containing 176 acres. Catherine, wife of John Ulrich released dower.

T:385-387. Robert Flora recorded deed 6 Nov. 1773 from Benjamin Sweet for £32..10, part of *Sideling Hill,* on west side of Sidling Hill Creek, being the remaning part of said tract not conveyed to Ignatius Thompson. Signed by mark. Martha, wife of Benjamin released dower.

T:387-390. Conrad Hersh recorded deed 6 Oct. 1773 from Paul Woolfe in consideration of 100 acres of land and £16 Pennsylvania, he assigns and confirms parcel called *Hershes Second Purchase,* part of *Resurvey on Mackey's Chance,* beginning at tract called *The Forrest,* taken up by Doct. Charles Carroll, containing 116 acres. Signed Paul Wolfe, before Jos Wood, Wm Bentley.

T:390-392. Martin Waltz recorded deed 6 Oct 1773 from Elias Bruner of Frederick Town, for £200 Pennsylvania, sells lot #48 Signed before Thos Price, William Beatty. Alverdeeny Bruner, wife of Elias Bruner, released dower right.

T:392-395. John Hughes recorded deed 6 Oct. 1774 [sic] made 7 Sept. 1773, from Calder Haymond of Bartley County, Virginia, tract called *Williams Lot,* containing 78 acres. For £100. Eleanor Haymond released dower.

T:395-399. Normand Bruce recorded deed 6 Oct. 1773 from Sarah Shaw, widow. Whereas Joseph Ogle, late of Frederick County, by his will, 18 April 1756 bequeath all his real estate to be divided between his children, allowing to his wife, Sarah Ogle, now Sarah Shaw, as much as two of his children, and Sarah, after his decease intermarried with a certain Adam Henry and during his life time, he and Sarah, together with the survivors, made division of said Joseph Ogle in the year 1767, and obtained out of his estate part of *Peace and Plenty,* containing 200 acres more or less. Since the division of his lands, the said Adm Henry died, and by his will did bequeath unto his wife, Sarah Henry, now Sarah Shaw, all his estate both real and personal, now Sarah for £300 hath bargained to the said Norman Bruce, tract called *Peace and Plenty,* containing 200a cres, except for that sold to a certain Ann Collins, in 1773.Signed by mark.

T:399-402. Edward Magruder recorded deed 6 Oct. 1773, from John Magruder, for £59 tract called *Magruder's Purchase,* originally called *Friendship;* and the other called *Addition to Magruder's Purchase,* for 59 acres. Signed before William Deakins Junr., Adam Stewart. Jane Magruder, wife of John released dower right.

T:402-404. Benjamin Veatch recorded deed 4 Oct. 1773 from Thomas Cramphin of Prince George's County, for £39..18 tract called *Pickleton's Rest,* containing 80 acres of land.

T:404-406. John Gabby recorded deed 6 Oct. 1773 from James Brownlee for £100 sells tract *Scant of Timber,* being part of tract *Rich Barrance,* patented to a certain Peter Shers, for 100 acres.

T:407-409. William Hawker recorded deed 6 Oct. 1773 from Benjamin Veatch for £112..15 sells part of *Pickleton's Rest,* 77 ½ acres. Ester Veatch released right of dower.

T:409-411. Daniel Keaver recorded deed 6 Oct. 1773 from Daniel Dulaney and Walter Dulaney, executors of Daniel Dulaney deceased. For £70 assigns parcel called *The Green Meadow,* 100 acres of land.

T:412-414. Daniel Wise recorded deed 6 Oct 1773, from Philip Rodenpiller, weaver, for £50, parcel called *Philip Rodenpiller's Ramble,* containing 150 acres. At the same time the wife of Philip Rodenpiller (not named) examined apart, released dower.

T:414-417. David Davis recorded deed 16 Oct. 1773 from Geo. Fredk Kindley. [Maringal note, examined and delivered David Davis 9 July 1781]. For £150 assigns tract called *Duvall's Forrest,* containing 100 acres more or less. Signed by mark.

T:417-419. Paul Woolfe recorded deed 6 Oct. 1773 from Conrad Kersh for 100 acres of land, by way of exchange, grants unto Paul Woolf, tract called *Hershes Purchase,* formerly conveyed to the said Conrad Hersh by the said Paul Woolf, containing 100 acres more or less. Signed by mark. T420 is blank page – END OF LIBER T

LIBER U

U:1-3. Robert Flora recorded deed 6 Oct. 1773 from Thomas Flora for £11..10, *Flora's Choice,* begins 25 perches from Potomac River, 3 miles below Sideling Hill Creek, 50 acres. Signed mark before Sam'l Beall Jr., John Stull.

U:3-5. [Marginal note: delivered Jacob Hesse, 25 May 1780.] Jacob Hess, joiner, recorded deed 6 Oct. 1773 from Thaddeus Beall for £100 sterling, lot in Georgetown, beg. At lot #13, adjacent to lots 9 & 10. Signed before William Deakins, Jr., Adam Steuart. Amelia Beall, wife of Thaddeus, released dower. AF paid Wm Murdoch Beall.

U:6-10. Christian Kingery, late of Lancaster County, Pennsylvania, recorded deed 6 Oct. 1773 from John Hartness for £100 sells land as son and heir at law of Robert Hartness Sr., deceased, part of *Perry's Retirement,* patented by Joseph Perry 29 Sept. 1754. M&B to division line of John Gabby's part. Elizabeth Hartness, widow of Robert and mother of John, released dower.

U:10-13. Abraham Ferree of Lancaster County, Pennsylvania, recorded deed 6 Oct 1773 from Evan Shelby for £35, *Shelby's Delight,* patented 19 April 1763, for 40 acres.

U:14-16. Jacob Winroad recorded deed 6 Oct 1773 from Adam Karr (Carr) for £350, part of *Brooke Grove Resurveyed,* for 150 acres. Hannah wife of Adam Karr released dower.

U:16-18. Martin Winters recorded deed 6 Oct 1773 from Edward Stocksdale of Baltimore County, for £100, *Stocksdell's Hills,* 100 acres. Signed by mark before Michael Hibner, John Crockett. Catherine, wife of Edward Stockdell released dower.

U:18-23. Christian Kingery, late of Lancaster County, mason, recorded deed 6 Oct. 1773 from John Hartness, son and heir of Robert Hartness, Sr., deceased, for £130 Pennsylvania, sells three small parcels, parts of *Resurvey on Well Taught,* containing 21 acres, 9 3/4 acre adjacent to *Perry's Retirement,* and 19 3/4 acres. Elizabeth Hartness, widow, released dower.

U:23-35. Normand Bruce recorded bill of sale 6 Oct. 1773 from James Young for £48..16, one black horse, one red cow, one black cow, six sheep, one pair smith's bellows. If sum paid with interest sale is void.

U:25-31. Thomas Cramphin recorded mortgage 9 Oct. 1773 from William McKay for two tracts, *William's Discovery,* and *McKays Chance,* adjacent to *Resurvey on Strife Ended,* together 493 3/4 acres. If sum with interest, paid by 10 Oct. 1774, this is void. Signed before Robert Peters, Adam Steuart.

U:31. Nathan Haines recorded release of mortgage 14 Oct. 1773 from Charles Carroll, barrister, executor and heir at law of within named Charles Carroll. Release of mortgage on tract *Cornwall,* 219 acres.

U:31-32. Joseph Anderson of Northampton County, Pennsylvania, recorded bill of sale 11 Sept. 1773 from James Anderson of Elizabeth Town, for £107..10..9, one servant man named Thomas, one slave named Nan, two feather beds and furniture. Signed before William Baird.

U:32-34. William Murdoch Beall recorded bill of sale 20 Oct. 1773 from John Ballenger for 5 shillings and further sum of £29..11.9, a debt due, sells crop of tobacco of tobacco house and all right to plantation laeased to me by Beall Bordley. Signed by mark before Thos Price, Laurence O'Neal.

U:34-37. Edward Burgess recorded deed 20 Oct 1773, made 20 Sept. from Humphrey Peddicord of Anne Arundel Co., for £243..15, two tracts, called *Silent Valley,* and *Baynes Good Luck.* For *Silent Valley,* beginning near the head of a branch which runs into Middle Bennett Creek, containing 80 acres. For *Bayne's Good Luck,* beginning at end of 5th line, laid out for 123 acres. Signed before Charles Jones, David Lynn. Rachel his wife released dower rights.

U:37-41. Mordecai Boone recorded deed 22 Oct. 1773 from Anthony Holmead for £329..16, all those parts of tracts called *The James,* and *Addition to the James,* that were not conveyed to Colmore Beanes, Samuel Turner and Alexander Clagett, containing 530 acres; also for further sum of £66, another tract called *Discovery,* on south side of a branch that falls into Watts Branch, for 100 acres. Susanna Holmead released dower.

U:41-44. Michael Hoover recorded deed 24 Oct. 1772 from Christopher Shockey for £50 indenture to rectify deed recorded in Liber M:500 which was acknowledged before only one Justice of the Peace. *Resurvey on Sarah's Delight.* Mary Shockey released dower.

U:44-45. William McGrath recorded bill of sale 22 Oct. 1773 from Elizabeth Carpenter for £16, one cow, one bull calf, one yearling, one year old bull, one steer, one horse and three hogs. Signed by mark before Benjamin Sedwick.

U:45-46. Jacob Byer and Christian Weaver recorded release of dower 24 Oct. 1773 from Elizabeth Dorsey of Anne Arundel County, for lot in Frederick Town, sold by her husband some time past. Witnesses: John Burgess Jr., Wm Dorsey.

U:46-49. Jacob Shockey recorded deed 24 Oct. 1773 from Christopher Shockey, for £50, part of *Third Resurvey on Sarah's Delight,* to correct errors in acknowledgment of previous deed recorded in liber M:530-531, which was only acknowledged before one Justice of the Peace, and two are required. Mary Shockey released dower rights.

U:49-53. John Shockey recorded deed 24 Oct. 1773 from Christopher Shockey, to correct errors in acknowledgment of previous deed recorded in liber M:557-558, which was only acknowledged before one Justice of the Peace, and two are required.

U:53-56. Valentine Shockey recorded deed 24 Oct. 1773 from Christopher Shockey, to correct errors in acknowledgment of previous deed recorded in liber M:560-561, which was only acknowledged before one Justice of the Peace. Mary Shockey released dower rights.

U:56-60. Philip Stambach recorded deed 24 Oct. 1773 from Christopher Shockey, to correct errors in acknowledgment of previous deed recorded in liber M:562-564, which was only acknowledged before one Justice of the Peace. Mary Shockey released dower rights.

U:60-64. John PickleHammer recorded lease 24 Oct. 1773 from Alexander Thomas Hawkins for 200 acre part of *Hawkins Merry Peep A Day,* to dividing line of tract with John Stone Hawkins, for lives of John Pickle Hammer, Ann Pickle Hammer his wife and Samuel Pickle Hammer their son. Signed before Thomas Gantt Jr. and Alexander Howard Magruder.

U:64-68. Richard Henderson of Bladensburg, Prince Georges County, recorded bill of sale 26 Oct. 1773 from Thomas James Sr. for debt due him of £35..6, and whereas Hugh Smith Dunn, of Frederick County, school master, has undertaken to make satisfaction for debt; for £30..14..6, Thomas James conveys to him one old bay horse, one cow and calf, one cow and yearling, 2 year old heifer, one steer, one sow, three barrows, two feather beds, furniture,b edseads and cords, 2 large chests, one small chests, all my pewter plates, dishes, basins, spoons, knives, iron pots, pans, my crop of tobacco and share of crop of corn, and assignment of lease on the plantation. Assignment of lease from Thomas James to Hugh Smith Dunn, consented to for remainder of time by Archibald Beall. Witnesses Alexander Beall, Samuel Beall.

U:68-70. James Marshall recorded deed 22 Oct. 1773 from George Fraser Hawkins of Prince George's County. Whereas Fielder Gantt by mortgage, two tracts, *The Mistaken Rival,* and *Gantt's Garden,* offered at public sale, and James Marshall was high bidder at £210 for *Gantt's Garden,* deed made.

U:71-72. John Glassford & Co. Recorded sale 1 Nov. 1773 from William Needham, indebted for £346..10..5, deliveres to Robert Ferguson, factor for John Glassford & Co., the following Negroes, Jim, Richard, Phillis and Poll. Signed before Robert Peter, Andrew Heugh.

U:73-77. John Glassford & Co., merchants in that part of Great Britain called Scotland, recorded mortgage 1 Nov. 1773 from David John Oden, indebted for £208..1..2, from dealings in store in Georgetown, mortgages tract called *Boys lot,* a part of *Fellowship,* deeded to him by Alexander Urquhart, 29 Oct. 1768, beginning at draught of Brooks Branch, which falls into Whetstone Branch, which falls into Seneca Creek, containing 141 ½ acres. Also Negro woman Phillis and Negro girl Margaret or Pegg; provided nevertheless that if sum paid with interest sale is void. David John Oden appoints Henry Riddle of Prince Georges County, attorney for Glassford & Co.

U:78-81. Alexander Thomas Hawkins of Prince George's County, recorded lease 3 Nov. 1773 from John Zear for £60 released 200 acres of *Hawkins Merry Peep a Day,* adjacent to *John and Sarah,* leased in 1768 on lives of John Zear, Barbara Zear his wife and Christian, their son.

U:81-82. Henry Petre recorded bill of sale 5 November 1773 from George Frederick Keber, for £6..3, one cow, one heifer and one calf. Signed before Jos Johnson, J.M. Widmyer, 11 Oct.

U:82-84. Alexander Thomas Hawkins recorded release 3 Nov. 1773 from Peter Lessley in possession of 200 acre part of *Hawkins Merry Peep A Day,* for lives of Peter Lessey, Susanna his wife and Solomon Lessy, son, for 5 shillings he surrenders their interest.

U:84-87. Henry Kenser recorded deed 8 Nov. 1773 from Catherine McKinley and Benjamin McKinley for £33, tract *Translvania,* contining 120 acres. Signed before Wm Blair, Ninian Chamberlain.

U:87-90. Edward Stevenson recorded deed 8 Nov. 1773 from Moses Ferree for £505 sells tract, *Strawberry Plains,* formerly in Baltimore County, for 100 acres. Sarah, wife of Moses Ferree released dower.

U:90-92. Walter Beall recorded trust deed 8 Nov. 1773 from Simon Shaffer for 5 shillings, for speedy payment of debts, to wit: Thomas Richardson, £25; John Barnes and Thomas Howe Ridgate, £51..7; John Glasford & Co., £14..9; William Molleson, £25; Notley Mattox, 19..9;

Jacob Upright, £19..10; assigns one horse, one mare, one cow and calf, 10 hogs, all wheat growing at late plantation, all his blacksmith's tools, and household furniture, except for his bed, to use to pay debts pro rata if not enough, or if overplus, balance to go back to Simon Shaffer.

U:93-94. Benjamin Higdon recorded lease 11 Nov. 1773 from William Brown for rents and considerations, leases his part of *Mill Seat,* 50 acres, according to a deed from Samuel Beall Jr., paying 20 shillings the first year and £5 thereafter annually. Signed both parties before Andrew Heugh, Elizabeth Heugh.

U:95-96. Colin Dunlap, and sons, merchants of Glasgow in Scotland, recorded bill of sale 17 Nov. 1773 from Bennett Neale, in consideration of a debt due and 5 shillings, assigns all my stock of grain, wheat, indian corn, one Negro named Richard, two cows, one black horse, and all my household furniture. Signed before Edward Burgess.

U:96-99 William Murdoch Beall recorded deed 23 Nov. 1773 from Joshua Burton for £76 sells part of tract called *Resurvey on Content,* containing 53 acres more or less, together with a second part containing together 96 acres. Signed by mark before Thos Price, Thos Price Junr.

U:99-102. Doctor Thomas Pollhouse recorded deed 28 Nov. 1773 from John Creal and Jacob Kiger, carpenters, for £15 sells lot #2 in Additional Lots of Frederick Town.

U:102-105. Jacob Smith recorded deed 8 Nov. 1773 from Henry Shover for £35 assigns 50 acres, part of 200 acres conveyed to him by Fielder Gannt, for part of *Fielderia Manor.* Ann Shover released dower right.

U:105-107. William Summers recorded deed 8 Nov. 1773 from Joseph Newton Chiswell for £60, part of *Second Resurvey on Wolf Cow,* 50 acres. Signed before Thomas Price, Upton Sheridine.

U:107-109. John Gaither Jr. recorded deed 8 Nov. 1773 from John Gaither Sr. & Agnes, his wife (Clare Agnes Rogers) of Anne Arundel County, for £50, tract *John and Jean's Chance,* for 200 acres. Signed before David Lynn, Edward Burgess.

U:110-114. Thomas Cramphin Jr. Recorded deed 8 Nov. 1773 from John Garrett Sr. for £400 tract called *Hermitage,* at Garrett's Spring Branch, which falls into Watry Branch of Rock Creek, where the main road now crosses, 197 acres. Signed by mark before Adam Steuart, William Deakins, Sr. Elizabeth Garrett released dower.

U:114-116. Jacob Hess of Georgetown, recorded deed 8 Nov. 1773 from Saml Hawkins Bayne of Prince George's County, for £30, sells one half part of lot #3 in Addition to Georgetown/ Signed before John Read Magruder, Alexander Symmes, J.P.s of PGC.

U:116-119. William Summers recorded deed 8 Nov. 1773 from Solomon Simpson, for £112..6, tract called *Wheat's Purchase,* lying at the Buck Lodge branch, containing 100 acres. Dorcas Simpson released dower.

U:120-122. Michael Minser recorded deed 8 Nov. 1773 from John Scott for £100, tract *Resurvey on Burkett's Lot,* 15 acres. Signed by mark before Wm Baird, John Stull. Christiana wife of John Scott released dower.

U:122-125. Richard Lilley recorded deed 8 Nov. 1773 from Joseph Wood, executor of Samuel Wickham, late of Frederick County, deceased for £120, sells tract called *Mount Pleasant,* a resurvey on land called *Lilly's Lot,* for 100 acres.

U:126-128. Henry Matthews recorded deed 8 Nov. 1773 from John Brown for £176 part of William Anderson's part of *Resurvey on Brooke's Resurvey,* made over to John Brown by John McMachon, 111 acres. Elizabeth Brown released dower.

U:129-131. Jacob Young recorded deed 8 November 1773 from Michael Bayer for £50, tract called *Michael's Lick,* adjacent to *Friendship,* 25 ½ acres.

U:132-135. Jacob Young recorded deed 8 November 1773 from Michael Bayer for £100 tract called *Trembling,* 100 acres.

U:135-138. Samuel Stover recorded deed 8 Nov. 1773 from Jacob Morningstar for £204 Pennsylvania, sells tract *Friendship,* part of *Keep Trieste,* beginning at 3rd line of *Park Hall,* 103 acres. Sarah wife of Jacob Morningstar released dower.

U:138-140. Bernard Johnson recorded deed 8 Nov. 1773 from John Rideout of Annapolis, for £39, part of tract called *Chatham,* containing 130 acres. Mary wife of John Rideout released dower.

U:141-143. Andrew Corelle (Korelle) of Lancaster County, Pennsylvania, recorded deed 8 November 1773 from Edward Lingan Head for £370, assigns *Mitchell's Fancy,* 100 acres. Prisciller, wife of Edward Lingan Head released dower.

U:143-145. Peter Erb Jr. Recorded deed 8 Nov. 1773 from Peter Erb Sr. For £30, assigns *Resurvey on Michael's Lot,* granted him 24 June 1764 for 83 acres, likewise a contiguous tract called *Leonards Lot,* 26 acres, sold by Jacob Banker 7 March 1761 on draught of Great Pipe Creek.

U:146-151. Joseph Moyer recorded deed 8 Nov. 1773 from Andrew Arnold for £900 Pennsylvania, sells three parcels, *Uncles Favor,* 100 acres; *Resurvey on Uncles Gift,* 123 ½ acres, and part of *Resurvey on Dawson's Purchase,* 171 ½ acres, adjacent o *Forrest of Needwood,* belonging to John Hawkins Jr. Signed by mark. Catherine Arnold released dower.

U:151-154. Frederick Black recorded deed 8 Nov. 1773 from John Martin for £81, tract called *The Company,* 100 acres. Margaret wife of John Martin released dower.

U:154-157. John Correlle of Lancaster County, Pennsylvania, recorded deed 8 Nov. 1773 from Andrew Correlle (Korelle) and Elizabeth his wife, for £307, part of *Michael's Fancy,* on west side of Beaver Dam Run, 100 acres. Signed before Joseph Wood, John Creager.

U:157-160. Peter Erb Jr. Recorded deed 8 Nov. 1773 from Peter Erb Sr. for £30, *Erb's Lot,* part of *High Germany,* on south side of Great Pipe Creek, adjacent to tracts *Wild Cat Spring,* and *James' Fancy,* 212 acres.

U:160-163. Matthew Logan recorded deed 8 Nov. 1773 from Abraham Milton, son and heir of Isaac Milton, deceased, for £45, tract *Milton's Paradice,* adjacent to *Frenchman's Purchase.*

U:163-167. John Rohrer recorded deed 8 Nov. 1773 from Yost Gardiner for £50, *Dorothy's Lot,* part of a resurvey called *Scared from Home,* containing 50 acres. Anna Gardner released dower rights.

U:167-170. Samuel Hawkins Beane recorded deed 8 Nov. 1773 from Chas Beatty & George Fraser Hawkins of Prince George's County, for £3, sells half part of lot #3 in Addition to Georgetown. Susanna Freeman, wife of G.F. Hawkins, released dower right before John Baynes, Thomas Clagett. Martha Beatty released dower before Wm Beatty, Thomas Price.

U:170-173. Peter Frank recorded lease 8 Nov. 1773 from Rudolph Etchicher/Aitcher for £16 and rents and covenants herein, assigns lot #37 on southwest side of Main St. in Westminster, south of land belonging to William Winchester, 1/4 of an acre. Part of *White's Levels.* Signed before Enoch Davis. Acknowledged before justices of Baltimore County, Wm Buchanan, Wm Spear.

U:173-175. Peter Butman recorded deed 8 Nov. 1773 from Philip Rodenpeeler for £16 for part of *Philip Rodenpeeler's Ramble by Quaker Tricks,* 40 ½ acres. Rachel Rodenpeeler released dower.

U:175-178. Benjamin McKinley recorded deed 8 Nov. 1773 from Abraham Milton, son and heir of Isaac Milton of Kent County, deceased, for £28, 30 acre part of *Milton's Paradice,* adjacent to Matthew Logan's part, and *Frenchman's Purchase.*

U:178-181. John Keller recorded deed 8 Nov. 1773 from Andrew Smith and Elizabeth Smith, his wife for £260, *Resurvey on part of Ramshorn,* 100 acres.

U:181-184. Teter Barnett, blacksmith, recorded deed 8 Nov. 1773 from Ulrich Bruner, for £44, part of *Badham Refuse,* near Israel Cabbin's Branch that falls into the Potomack, 47 acres. Franah Bruner released dower.

U:184-187. Michael Spacer, taylor, recorded deed 8 Nov. 1773 from Conrad Hartsock for £120, *Laine's Choice,* on west side of mountain that leads to Beaver Creek, a draught of Antietam, 50 acres. Wife on Conrad Hartsock (not named) released dower.

U:187-190. Joshua Dellaplaine recorded deed 8 Nov. 1773 from Cornelius Carmack for £300, *Resurvey on Welch Cabbin,* in the 8 line of Major Joseph Wood's part, th 184 acres. Margery, wife of Cornelius released dower.

U:190-194. Nathan Holland recorded lease 17 Nov. 1773 from Jno Worthington Warfield of Anne Arundel County, for yearly rents and covenants, tract *Warfields Vinyard,* on Burton's Cabbin Branch of Bennett's Creek, 270 acres for 21 years, to settle two plantations, and to build on each a framed dwelling house, 24x16, a bastard framed tobacco house, 40x20, to plant a 100 tree apple orchard. Signed by both parties.

U:194-198. John Glassford & Co. Recorded mortgage 8 Nov. 1773 from Walter Smith Greenfield, for £365..6..5, Negro men Sampson, Tim, and Sharper; Negro girls Cloe and Grace and their increase; one brindle cow, one black yearling, one read cow and brindle heifer, other livestock and horses enumerated. If sum paid sale is void. Signed before Robert Peter.

U:199-202. Alexander Thomas Hawkins of Prince Georges County, recorded lease 17 Nov. 1773 from Christian Nieswanger for rents and covenants, leases 200 acres of *Hawkins Merry Peep a Day.*

U:202-203. John Musgrove recorded bill of sale 17 Nov. 1773. I am indebted for £50 , assigns bay horse, sorrel mare, seven head of sheep, three head of cattle, 30 hogs, 2 feather beds and furniture, 2 iron pots, one frying pan and dutch oven, plates, pewter basin, other personalty, all tobacco I now possess. If sum paid, sale void. Signed Peter Pearce before John Riggs, Thomas Riggs.

U:203-205. John Campbell, factor of George Buchanan and Andrew Buchanan, merchants of Glascow in Scotland, recorded bill of sale 17 Nov. 1773 from Joseph Sparrow for £60..5, sells two red cows, one red yearling, two black horses, crop of tobacco and crop of corn, five hogsheads of cider, cart and gears, feather bed, iron pot, Dutch oven, oak tabel and chest.

U:205-208. [marginal note: Delivered to Joseph Swearingen, brother of Benny Swearingen.] Benny Swearingen of Berkeley County, Virginia, recorded deed 18 Nov. 1773, from Levi Mills, for £6, assigns part of a tract called *Easy Got,* being a resurvey on *Antietam Bottom,* on the side of the Potomac River, 75 acres more or less. Elizabeth, wife of Levi Mills released dower.

U:209-210. John Dickerson recorded sale 18 Nov. 1773 from Suratt Dickerson for £100 sell 76 acres of land, called *John and James Choice,* and one Negro man, named Charles, 4 feather beds and furniture, 2 horses, 16 sheep, 25 hogs, 3 cows and calves, 2 heifers, 2 steers, 3 iron pots, 2 dishes, 3 basins, 17 plates, cider crock, woolen wheel, linen wheel, crop of tobacco and wheat, provided nevertheless if sum paid by Dec. 1774, sale is void.

U:210-211. Thomas Wilson recorded sale 19 Nov 1773 from James Wilson for £38..1..8, sells all my crop of corn and tobacco, three horses, two cows and calves, two hogs and all my household furniture. Putting him in full possession by delivery of one gray mare. Signed before Andrew Heugh, John Abington.

U:211-215. Henry Walters, tanner, recorded deed 20 Nov 1773 from Jacob Hoover, saddle tree maker. Whereas 17 August 1766, between Daniel Dulaney of the City of Annapolis, unto Jacob Hoover, lot #265, in Additional Lot to Frederick Town, for £63 Henry Walters agrees to purchase. Christiner, wife of Jacob Hoover released dower.

U:215-218. Thomas Frazier recorded deed 22 Nov. 1773 from Thomas Gantt Jr. of Prince George's County, for £365..3..4 part of *Hawkin's Merry Peep a Day,* M&B to division line between John Stone Hawkins and Alexander Thomas Hawkins, made by Alexander Magruder and Thomas Hawkins agreeable to the will of John Hawkins, laid out for 313 acres. Signed before John Cooke, Henry Webb. Susannah Gantt released dower rights.

U:218-222. Thomas Niell, merchant, recorded mortgage 4 Dec. 1773, from Robert Owen, merchant, for £946..3..7, three parts or parcels of land, part of *Brother,* containing 100 acres; 2 tract nd *Resurvey on Advantage,* 150 acres, and third parcel, part of *Discontent,* 100 acres. Signed before Thomas Price, Elias Barton.

U:222-226. [Marginal note, delivered to Jacob Gray, 12 Oct. 1784]. Jacob Gray of Petersburgh, York County, miller, recorded deed 23 Nov 1773 from Henry Brothers of the town of Petersburgh, township of Germany, County of York, Pennsylvania, carpenter, and his wife, Fronica. Whereas George Onstat, for consideration therein, sold to Henry Brother, parcel called *Rich Hill,* standing near Piney Run, containing 100 acres, recorded in Liber J:855-857. For £60 sold to Jacob Gray, containing 24 acres. Witnesses Archibald McClean, and in G.S., not identified. Acknowledged before Andrew Heugh, David Lynn.

U:226-229. Zadock Dickerson recorded deed 4 Dec. 1773 from Surrat Dickerson for £79 part of *John and James Choice,* containing 79 acres.

U:229-235. Andrew Heugh recorded deed 7 Dec. 1773 from Capt. Henry Brooke of Prince George's County, for £111..15 part of tract, part of *Dan,* beginning at main run of Rock Creek Branch, at the beginning of *Forrest,* being the southernmost part of *Dan,* conveyed by Thomas Brooke Esq. and Barbara (his wife) unto his brother Clement Brooke, grandfather of the said Henry Brooke, for 500 acres. Adj. to part of land originally surveyed for Col. Henry Darnall, M&B for 243 acres, references deed in F:1322. Also a second part of *Dan,* containing 34 acres. Signed before Charles Hagarty, John F. A. Riggs. Lord Proprietor's Justices of the Provincial Court. Mary Brooke, wife of Henry Brooke, released dower.

U:235 Jacob Brookover recorded release of mortgage 8 Dec. 1773 from William M. Beall. Received of Jacob Brookover, £4..11..7 in full for the balance of his mortgage. Signed Wm M. Beall.

U:236 John Clary recorded bill of sale 29 Nov. 1773 from Francis Mercer of Frederick County, Virginia, make over my right to a sorrel horse, which horse is to go towards the payment for a lease which Devon Clary now lives on.

U:236-238. George Collins recorded lease 8 Nov. 1773 from John Wilcoxon, tract on Monocacy known as *Gunder's Delight,* 62 ½ acres, to hold for 61 years, the first two years rent free, and to work no more than his own family and two hired hands, and after two years to pay 1000 weight good and merchantable tobacco, delivered at Georgetown, for every year after. Signed John Wilcoxon, George Collins before Andrew Heugh, John F. A. Riggs.

U:238-242. Andrew Heugh and Robert Peter recorded trust deed 20 Nov. 1773 from William Needham, three parcels of land: part of a tract called *King Cole* of which the said Sarah Needham, deceased, was seized and has become the estate of said William Needham, part of tract called *Labyrinth,* lying between Charles Jones' part, and tract called *Forest,* also one other tract of land called *Needham's Discovery,* containing 11 acres, and all the Negroes, goods and chattels of him the said William Needham in trust and under the special confidcence, that they will offer same at public venue, and the money arising they will divide amongst the creditors of the said William Needham in discharge of their debts. Signed by all three parties before Charles Jones, Adam Steuart.

U:242-246. John Dorsey of Anne Arundel County, recorded mortgage 18 Nov. 1773 from Henry Barnes for £113..19..3 sterling, four lots being on *Chews Farm,* #10, #11, and one lot called *Mill Lot* and one called *Charles Barne's lot,* also one Negro woman called Rose, the unexpired time of two white servants named Richard Duffle and John Walker; one white horse, one bay blooded mare, one gray horse, one gray mare, six cows, two yearlings, 14 head of sheep; also four feather beds and furniture, all the crop of tobacco and crop of wheat. Signed in presence of Samuel Beall Junr., Upton Sheridine.

U:246-249. Chidley and Jno Matthews, sons and heirs of Samuel Matthews, deceased, recorded deed 23 Nov. 1773 from Samuel Beall Jr. For £80 part of tract called *Frenchman's Purchase,* containing 202 acres.

U:250-253. Jacob Huffman, taylor, recorded deed 23 Nov. 1773 from John Gomber, cooper, for £40 lot #30 conveyed to Valentine Shriner in Frederick Town, Signed John Gomber. Rachel Gomber released dower.

U:253-256. Moses Robinett recorded deed 23 Nov. 1773 from Edward, John and Joseph Perren, for sum of £10 tract called *Addition to the Two Springs,* containing 50 acres.

U:256-260. Archibald Shearer of Frederick County, Virginia, recorded deed 23 Nov. 1773 from David Ross of Prince George's County, for £50 tract called *Addition to Jack's Bottom,* lying on Potomac River, laid out for 52 acres. Ariana Ross released dower rights.

U:260-264. Charles Haass and Henry Landice of Lancaster County, Pennsylvania, recorded deed 23 Nov. 1773 from Abraham Welty for £1700 Pennsylvania, the following tracts on Sam's Creek, a draught of Little Pipe Creek, part of *Level Glade,* part of Resurvey on a tract called *The Deeps,* laid out for 87 acres and 8 acres; and a third parcel of 4 acres Margaline [sic] wife of Abraham Welty released dower rights.

U:264-267. Jacob Harbough recorded deed 23 Nov. 1773 from Casper Lockman for £15 tract called *Casper's Fours,* beginning at south side of the Kitoctin Mountain, and about 5 perches north of the Indian Run, 10 ½ acres. Signed G.S. Judiana, wife of Casper Lockman released dower rights.

U:267-270. Frederick Solar recorded deed 23 Nov. 1773 from Casper Lockman, blacksmith, for £33 assigns land in the South Mountain, on the head waters of Kittocton Creek, part of tract called *Junech,* containing 60 acres. Judiana Lockman released dower rights.

U:270-273. Philip Ambrose recorded deed 23 Nov. 1773 from Casper Lockman, blacksmith, for £123, assigns the following three tracts in the south mountain, on the head waters of branches of Kittocktin Creek, one called *Simpy Ridge,* for 9 acres; another called *Juneck,* for 30 acres; and third parcel of 125 acres more or less, Judiana, wife of Casper Lockman released dower rights.

U:274-277. John Willson recorded deed 23 Nov 1773. [Marginal note, exam'd & delivered Cornelius Willson, adm. Of Jno Willson]. Deed from Edward, John and and Joseph Perren, executors of John Perren, deceased, for £10 tract called *Second Addition to Two Springs,* 50 acres of land.

U:277-279. George Robinett recorded deed 23 Nov. 1773, from Edward, John and and Joseph Perren, executors of John Perren, deceased, for £50 tract called *Addition to Two Springs,* 100 acres of land.

U:280-283. Andrew Biddle recorded deed 23 Nov. 1773 from Samuel Cookson for £3, lot in town of New London, #7, southwest of main street. Mary, wife of Samuel Cookson released dower.

U:283-286. George Barnour recorded deed 23 Nov. 1773 from Samuel Cookson for £9, lot #50 in town of New London, south west of main streeet. Mary Cookson released dower.

U:286-292. Michael Troutman recorded deed 23 Nov. 1773 from Daniel Swaggert, for £500 part of tract, *Shady Grove,* on north side of Kittoctin Creek, containing 56 acres; made over from Christian Leatherman to Daniel Swaggert, 18 March 1763, and second part.

U:292-294. William Dennis recorded deed 25 Nov. 1773 from John Flint for £65 part of *Partnership,* on a branch of Little Seneca, 50 acres.

U:295-297. Samuel Blackmore recorded deed 23 Nov. 1773 from Robert Peter for £53..4..7 parcel called *Resurvey on Brandy,* containing 491 acres

U:297-300. Abraham Boyd and John Boyd recorded deed 23 Nov. 1773 from John Kennedy for 5 shillings sterling, tract called *Dantzik,* beginning at *Boyd's Delay,* for 144 acres.

U:300-304. Charles Carroll recorded land commission 20 Nov. 1773. To Messrs William Winchester, David Shriver, Edwd Lamb, and Edward Stevenson. Charles Carroll by his petition to perpetuate the bounds on *Hail's Luck,* was granted commission. Edward Lamb, one of the Commissioners within named being a Quaker, took a solemn affirmation to execute the same before Wm Buchanan of Baltimore County. The following depositions were taken: John Storum, about 50 years of age, deposed that Stephen Crise bought the said land called *Hails Luck,* at oak tree, and also deposed that Uncle Uncles, also ran land from same trees. Stephen Crise, about 52 years of age, agreed on beginning tree. [Above mentioned black oak tree stands on south side of Piney Run.]

U:304-308 Paul Road requested land commission and deposition recorded 20 Nov. 1773. To Messrs James Smith, Christian Ovendolph, Thomas Hawk and Samuel Baker, on tract called *Paul's Purchase.* Part of tract, *Resurvey on Root's Hill.* Deposition of Jacob Bruner, stated that Col. Thomas Prather, being called by Joseph Chapline to run the line of the *Resurvey on Root's Hill,* which began at a white oak tree in Andrew Pitman's meadow, the commissioners finding the stumps of the trees mentioned set up stones.

U:308-312. Christian Lower of Bucks County, Pennsylvania, recorded mortgage 26 Nov. 1773 from Nicholas Seybert, miller, by certain obligation for £2200 Maryland, due on 1st January 1784, to better secure payment, for £1100 sells a certain plantation in Frederick County, called *Norway,* for 300 acres of land with improvements, buildings, houses, barns, mills, out houses, etc.

U:312-315. Thomas Johnson recorded deed 23 Nov. 1773 from Thomas Duckett for £200, tract called *Flag Pond,* granted to Jacob Duckett, father of Thomas Duckett, adjacent to *Perry's Lot,* containing 321 ½ acres Mary, wife of Thomas Duckett released dower.

U:316-319. Joseph Wood Jr. recorded deed Nov. 1773 from Joseph Wood for £250 part of *Content,* a part of the *Resurvey on Welch's Cabbin,* containing 155 acres of land. Catherine, wife of Joseph Wood released dower.

U:319-322. Andrew Wolfe late of Chester County, Pennsylvania, recorded deed 23 Nov. 1773, from Abraham Rowland, for £430 all his right to tracts on the Grind Stone Branch of Great Pipe Creek, containing 100 acres, and tract called *Small Hopes,* adjacent to *Good Spring,* for 13 ½ acres. Catherine wife of Abraham Rowland released dower.

U:323-326. John Garrett recorded deed 23 Nov. 1773 from John Payne for £300. *Pain's Delight,* to dividing line with his brother, Phlail Payne's part of said land, containing 34 ½ acres. Mary, wife of John Payne released dower.

U:326-329. Charles Fair recorded deed 23 Nov. 1773 from Wm Diggs and Raphael Taney for £45, assign part of *Resurvey on Brother's Agreement,* containing 59 acres. Signed before Jno Reeder Junr., Henry Reeder. Elenor, wife of Raphael Taney and Catherine, wife of William Diggs released dower.

U:329-332. Robert Peter recorded deed 23 Nov 1773. [Marginal note: Exam'd & del'd Robert Peter 21 June 1779]. From Evan Shelby, for £30, parcel called *Pipe Tomahawk,* on north side of a hollow that leads to a run called Laince Run, a draught of Licken Creek, about 4 miles from Fort Frederick, containing 25 acres.

U:332-335. Evan Shelby recorded deed 23 Nov. 1773 from Samuel Postlethwaite of Cumberland County, Pennsylvania, for £25 Pennsylvania, sells tract called *Pipe Tomahawk,* 4 miles from Fort Frederick, 25 acres.

U:335-337. Mitchell and Gaither recorded bill of sale 23 Nov. 1773 from Nathan Barnes, indebted to Mitchell and Gaither, merchants of Baltimore and Frederick Counties, sells one sorrel mare, one small gray mare, signed before Richard Davis.

U:337-340. George Hockersmith recorded deed 23 Nov 1773 from Henry Williams for £30 a tract of land, now called *Hockersmith's Purchase,* part of a tract bequeathed unto Esther Williams, by will of John Williams, deceased, and afterwards sold by her to Henry Williams, beginning at second line of a tract called *Porter's First Addition,* now laid out for 25 acres. Signed before David Lynn, Andrew Heugh. Mary, wife of Henry Williams released dower.

U:341-344. John Karen recorded deed 23 Nov. 1773 from Joseph Chapline & Henry Coleman for £100 confirms part of *Resurvey on Tom's Gift,* 120 acres. Mary, wife of Henry Coleman relinquished dower right.

U:344-347. Andrew Rough recorded deed 23 Nov. 1773 from Samuel Beall Jr., for £120, part of *Frenchman's Purchase,* containing 300 acres.

U:348-350. Philip Henry Thomas recorded deed 23 Nov. 1773 from Thomas Duckett, executor of Jacob Duckett, his father, who directed him to sell tract called *the Mountain,* 28 acres, for £10..10, containing 28 acres more or less.

U:350-353. Colin Dunlap & Son, merchants of Glasgow, recorded mortgage 27 Nov. 1773 from Francis King for £67..19..9 one red roan horse, one bay mare, one brown mare colt, two red cows, one pyed cow, bought at Vatchel Davis's sale the 22nd instant; one ton shod waggon; three feather beds with all the cloaths, and a suit of curtains, a large looking glass with all the rest of my household furniture, also my crops of tobacco and wheat, provided always that if sum paid with interest this shall be void. Signed before Robert Peter, John Dunlop.

U:354. Negro Margaret recorded manumission 18 Dec. 1773 from Nathan Haines, from this date. Signed 1st day, third month, March, 1771. Before Wm Roberts (signed by mark), Elizabeth Roberts (by mark), Allen Farquhar, Jr.

U:355-359. John Ramsburgh recorded mortgage 16 Dec. 1773, from Jacob Shuh. Whereas the said John Ramsburgh became security for the said Jacob Shuh, in a bond to Peter Bruner for £100, and also two bonds to Mary Peckenpough for £8 and £13, for securing the payment and for 5 shillings, he assigns 125 acres more or less, part of *Resurvey on PawPaw Bottom,* Barbary, wife of Jacob Shuh released dower.

U:359-363. Casper Mantz recorded deed 17 Dec. 1773 from Eleanor Charlton of Frederick Town, widow, executor of Arthur Charlton, deceased, who directed that lot #34 be divided and sold, for purposes stated within will, at public sale. Casper Mantz was high bidder at £177, for a share of lot #34 in Frederick Town, on Main Street.

U:363-367. Francis Meredith recorded deed 17 Dec. 1773 from Amos McGinley and Ann his wife. Whereas by indenture of release from Charles Carroll to Amos McGinley, for part of *Carroll's Delight,* for £100 sterling, sells part adjacent to Charles McAllister's land, to Alexander Adams' corner, to corner of Samuel Knox's. 144 1/4 acres.

U:367-370. William Douglas recorded deed 17 Dec 1774, [made 1 Nov. 1773] from Jacob Walker for £38 Pennsylvania, tract, *Works Easy,* Elizabeth, wife of Jacob Walker released dower.

U:370-373. John Twieg recorded deed 17 Dec. 1773, from Edward Perrin, John Perrin and Joseph Perrin for £25, tract beginning near Old Town Creek, for 50 acres.

U:373-377. Elias Major recorded deed 17 Dec. 1773, made 26 June 1773 from Charles Ridgely of Baltimore County, eldest son and heir of John Ridgely, merchant, for £257, part of *Bond's Meadow*, on west side of *Hazard,* 178 acres. Signed before John Griffith, Richard Cromwell. Rebecca Ridgely, wife of Charles, released dower.

U:377-380. Ludwick Miller recorded deed 17 Dec. 1773 from John Middlecalf, part of tract called *Will's Forest,* on Meadow Branch of Great Pipe Creek, same tract conveyed by John Middlekauff to Ludwick Miller and recorded in Liber O:258-259; 92 acres.

U:380-381. Peter Ferree of Lampeter Twp., Lancaster Co., recorded bond 13 Dec. 1773 from Paul Sipe (Seib) for £130 empowers him to act as attorney to sue and receive payments. Signed by mark.

U:382-384. Jacob Zimmerman recorded deed 25 Dec 1773 from Daniel Leatherman for £5, tract *Nazareth,* 82 acres.

U:385-388. Ludwick Miller recorded deed 17 Dec. 1773 from John Middlekauf for £50, part of *Resurvey on Shear Spring,* on Meadow Branch of Great Pipe Creek. 63 acres.

U:388-391. Jacob Mills recorded deed 17 Dec. 1773 from Isaac Shelby, for £40, Pennsylvania, tract called *What's Left,* near a small branch that falls into Lickin Creek, at lower end of Jacob Mills' plantation. 79 ½ acres.

U:391-395. Michael Eichenberger recorded deed 17 Dec. 1773 from Peter Coonce for £90, tract called *Hard Fortune*, part of *Resurvey on Parks Hall,* conveyed to him by Andrew Grim for 120 acres. Signed by mark. Wife not named released dower.

U:395-399. Sebastian Wigle recorded deed 17 Dec. 1773 from Eleanor Charlton of Frederick Town, widow, executor of Arthur Charlton, deceased, who directed that lot #34 be divided and sold, for purposes stated within will, at public sale. For high bid of £40..5, a part of division of lot #34 in Frederick Town, on Main Street.

U:399-402. Francis Mantz recorded deed 17 Dec. 1773 from Eleanor Charlton of Frederick Town, widow, executor of Arthur Charlton, deceased, who directed that lot #34 be divided and sold, for purposes stated within will, at public sale. For high bid of £102, a part of division of lot #34 in Frederick Town, on Main Street.

U:402-406. George Wise recorded deed 17 Dec. 1773 from Eleanor Charlton of Frederick Town, widow, executor of Arthur Charlton, deceased, who directed that lot #34 be divided and sold, for purposes stated within will, at public sale. For high bid of £47..10, a part of division of lot #34 in Frederick Town, on Main Street.

U:406-409. Martin Shoup recorded deed 17 Dec. 1773 Catharine Knave (Knouff) for £184..10, part of *Addition to Legacy,* 50 acres.

U:409-412. Thomas McElfresh recorded deed 17 Dec. 1773 from Greenberry Cheney Sr. of Prince George's County, for £40, *Chaney's Lot,* 50 acres.

U:412-415. David Spangler recorded deed 17 Dec. 1773, from John Middlecauff for £33, tract called *Wills Forest,* part of a resurvey on *Shear Spring,* on Meadow Branch a draught of Great Pipe Creek, 11 3/4 acres.

U:415 Christian Shirock recorded deed 17 Dec. 1773 from Jacob Coller (Gollar) for £3, two acres and 28 perches, part of tract called *Den of Wolves.* Signed by mark. Acknowledged before Thomas Price, John Stull. Alienation fine paid Wm M. Beall.
Last deed recorded. Signed
Geo M. Tyler
Apt. Clerk

INDEX

98 Frederick County Land Records

Catherine 24
Elias................................79
Franah 85
Henry............23, 39, 40, 41
Jacob 18, 89
Magdalena...........23, 40, 41
Margaret........................18
Peter 24, 91
Stephen...........................7
Ulrich 11, 85
Buchanan
Andrew....................32, 86
George.....................13, 86
John................................69
Wm.........................85, 89
Buckey
Mary...............................42
Peter 42
Buff
Michael 42, 44
Burch
Jestinian.........................56
Jonathan 23
Burchfield
Elizabeth 8
Robert...............................8
Burgee
Thomas.....................22, 38
Burgess
Basil 33, 44
Edward ... iv, 61, 69, 71, 77,
81, 83
John Jr.............................81
Mary........................... 61
Mary Davis.................... iv
Richd 78
Thomas........................ 22
Burgeys
Eleanor 22
Thomas 22
Burk
Edward 15
Wm 15
Burkett
Christopher....................31

Burton
Isaac 72
Joshua........................... 83
Sarah 72
Bush
Mathias..........................55
Butler
Mary..............................75
Peter 75
Richard 75
Butman
Peter 85
Butt /Butts/Putts/Potts
Annamaria......................67
Emerick 67
Ludwick 18, 47
Byer
Jacob 81
Bytesell
Henry.............................74
Caldwell
James...............................7
Calhoun
John................................78
Callaman
John................................48
Calvert
Benedict 74
Camp
Adam..............................74
Campbell
Aeneas/Eneas/Aens.. v, 6-8,
12-14, 16, 20, 22-25, 27,
28, 30, 39, 43, 47, 53, 67
John................................ 86
John Jr............................44
John Sr. 33, 44
Canade
Jno.................................39
Cannady
Isaac 52
Carlow
Henry...............................8
Carmack
Cornelius 70, 85
Levi 2

Margery.........................85
Carn (Karn)
Jacob 48
John................................67
Carpenter
Elizabeth 81
Carr
Moses.............................74
Carroll
Benjamin........................35
Charles ...... i, 11, 37, 42, 43,
50, 63, 64, 68, 78,80, 89,
91
Charles Jr 2, 3, 19
Daniel....................19, 44, 59
James..............................33
John 53
Carver
Samuel..............................9
Cassell
Jacob 14
Martin..........................1, 3
Castle
George............................24
Cecill
Joshua.............................60
Chamberlain
Abigail............................28
John 28
Ninian............................82
Chanefield
William 17
Chaney
Ann................................27
Charles 58
Charles Jr. 78
Zachariah.......................27
Chapline
James.........................v, 70
Joseph ...... v, 10, 12, 21, 41,
42, 69, 71, 89, 90
William v
William Williams............70
Charlton
Arthur..................74, 91, 92
Eleanor....................91, 92

Frederick County Land Records

Poplar Spring 24
Pork Hall 46
Porter's First Addition 90
Quench Orchard 33
Quince Orchard 48
Rattle Snake Denn..............43
Red Liquor 51
Resruvey on Longatepaugh ..
. ... 53
Resurvey on Beaver Dam
  Branch.....................65
Resurvey on Advantage 86
Resurvey on Anchor and
  Hope........................20
Resurvey on Andrews
  Chance 62
Resurvey on Antietam
  Bottom 70
Resurvey on Antietam Level
. ... 21
Resurvey on Arpos.............27
Resurvey on Batchelor's
  Delight 72, 76
Resurvey on Batchelor's
  Forest 38, 66
Resurvey on Batchelor's
  Hope 58, 65
Resurvey on Bayleys Fancy
 78
Resurvey on Beall's Meadow
 13
Resurvey on Beaver Dam
  Level 66
Resurvey on Benjamin's
  Luck 3
Resurvey on Benjamin's
  Square 11, 28
Resurvey on Black Acorn ..77
Resurvey on Black Oak Hill .
. ... 64, 65
Resurvey on Brandy...........89
Resurvey on Brooke's
  Resurvey 68, 84
Resurvey on Brother's
  Agreement.................28,
  32, 60, 66, 68, 90

Resurvey on Buck Field.... 20
Resurvey on Buck Range...35
Resurvey on Burkett's Lot . .
. ... 64, 83
Resurvey on Chaney's
  Delight 46
Resurvey on Charles Mount49
Resurvey on Chester ....
  ....20, 50, 52
Resurvey on Chevy Chase .73
Resurvey on Conten.3, 72, 83
Resurvey on Contentment..72
Resurvey on Cooper's Alley ..
 5
Resurvey on Dawson's
  Purchase 84
Resurvey on Dry Bottom ...14
Resurvey on Dutch's Folly
  ....72, 76
Resurvey on Egypt.............69
Resurvey on Forest 4
Resurvey on Forrest in Need
 4
Resurvey on Fountain Low....
 40
Resurvey on French's Lot..74
Resurvey on Friendship
  Dropt 13
Resurvey on Gabriel's
  Choice 3
Resurvey on George's
  Discovery..............43, 44
Resurvey on George's
  Mistake 73
Resurvey on Good Luck ...39
Resurvey on Good
  Neighborhood 64
Resurvey on Goodwill 4
Resurvey on Hager's Fancy
  ....58, 65
Resurvey on Hall'sChoice .47
Resurvey on Henry's Last
  Shift...........................59
Resurvey on Hibernia ..24, 51
Resurvey on Hickory
  Thickett.....................49

Resurvey on Hills and Dales .
. ... 70
Resurvey on Hortman's Place
. ...71
Resurvey on Ill Will............8
Resurvey on Isaac's Range . .
  ....51, 57
Resurvey on Jacob's Well . . .
. ... 10, 32
Resurvey on James' Fancy.36
Resurvey on Johnson's
  Levell 5
Resurvey on Joseph's
  Friendship 11, 62
Resurvey on Justice's Delight
 15
Resurvey on Lashmonts
  Folly............................52
Resurvey on Laugh and be
  Fat 4
Resurvey on Lewis Forrest . .
. ... 64, 70
Resurvey on Limestone Rock
. ... 16
Resurvey on Locust March .. i
Resurvey on Locust Neck
  ....13, 16, 17
Resurvey on Locust Thicket .
. ... 29
Resurvey on Logsdon's
  Amendment.................64
Resurvey on Long Bottom .36
Resurvey on Longatebough .
. ... 74
Resurvey on Longatepaugh ..
. ... 47, 66
Resurvey on Mackey's
  Chance 78
Resurvey on Mend All 19
Resurvey on Mendall 66
Resurvey on Merryland......41
Resurvey on Michael's Lot . .
. ... 84
Resurvey on Michael's
  Mistake 53

www.ingramcontent.com/pod-product-compliance
Lightning Source LLC
Chambersburg PA
CBHW080334270326
41927CB00014B/3220